Front cover
Charles I with M.de St Antoine (no.11)

Back cover
Portrait of the artist (no.65)

Sir Anthony van Dyck, self-portrait (detail from fig.33)

Oliver Millar

Van Dyck in England

National Portrait Gallery, London

Contents

Published for the exhibition held
from 19 November 1982 to 20 March 1983
at the National Portrait Gallery, London

Exhibition Organiser Malcolm Rogers
Exhibition Designer Joe Pradera

© Sir Oliver Millar, 1982
ISBN 0 904017 48 6
Published by the National Portrait Gallery,
London WC2H OHE

Catalogue edited by Mary Pettman

Designed by Graham Johnson

Printed in England by Lund Humphries,
London and Bradford

Foreword

Van Dyck, steeped in the European tradition, above all in the work of Titian and Veronese, set the art of portraiture in this country on an entirely new course. His style, his elegance and his repertory of designs were to exert a profound influence on subsequent British painting; Gainsborough, who shared his technical dexterity and brilliance, idolized him. More dazzlingly precocious than Lawrence, with an output as prodigious as that of Reynolds, it comes as a shock to realize that he was no more than forty-two at his death. Unlike his master, Rubens, Gladstonian in virility and stamina, Van Dyck was far from robust; he was highly strung, restless, neurotic, sometimes difficult, essentially withdrawn, qualities which his extraordinary charm and brilliance held in uneasy balance. Whereas the essence of Rubens lay in opulence or in drama on a heroic scale, the essence of Van Dyck's spirit lay in *poesie*. The beautiful and deeply moving *Cupid and Psyche* (no.58) is among his masterpieces. Similarly, in his portrayal of the Christian story, his imagination was quickened by the more poignant episodes: the moment of Our Lord's betrayal rather than His flagellation, the lamentation over the dead Christ rather than the deposition from the Cross; in his many renderings of the Madonna with the Child Jesus he is infinitely tender. This introspection, a certain melancholy, a consciousness of the fragility of human endeavour and of life itself, informs his portraits, the genre upon which his reputation has rested. Van Dyck, always so susceptible to atmosphere, was undoubtedly the perfect artist to reflect the brittle fabric of Caroline society on the eve of Civil War; so much so that, in our minds, the two have become synonymous and, in this exhibition, the mood of an epoch is recreated.

But, in making this identification, we should not forget that Van Dyck was a painter of international renown; one of the unanswered questions is why he remained so long in England. Five years in Italy and five in his native Antwerp intervened between his first visit to the Stuart court and his longer period of residence in London. The great full-lengths of the Brignole Sale family in Palazzo Rosso in Genoa are the most accessible of his Italian portraits which retain something of their original sumptuous, yet sombre, setting; but the hauteur with which he endowed his Italian sitters may be studied nearer at home in the *Emanuel Philibert of Savoy* at Dulwich. For the distinction of his second Flemish style one turns to the masterly *Philippe Le Roy* in the Wallace Collection. Both his approach to portraiture and the range of his patterns were established before the English years. Yet never were they more prodigally displayed than in those years.

For the selection of the exhibition his fellow Trustees and I are once again indebted, as in the case of *Sir Peter Lely* (1978–9), to Sir Oliver Millar, Surveyor of The Queen's Pictures and the leading authority on seventeenth-century British painting, from whom I have drawn a number of the foregoing observations. As Sir Oliver points out, Van Dyck's legacy was such that no exhibition could be more fundamental to one of this Gallery's principal purposes, the study of British portraiture. His detailed catalogue, which combines sensitivity with scrupulous scholarship, is richly informative, a major contribution to our knowledge and understanding of Van Dyck, his style, his technique and methods of work, his place in contemporary art and in English society. Sir Oliver makes his acknowledgements elsewhere; I warmly reiterate his thanks to Malcolm Rogers and my other colleagues, for without the devotion and enthusiasm of the Gallery staff no such complex enterprise as this would ever be possible. The space occupied by the exhibition is new, and for the successful completion of these galleries we are indebted to our colleagues in the Property Services Agency. Joe Pradera, as exhibition designer, has used this splendid new space with sympathy and ingenuity.

Her Majesty The Queen has graciously lent six paintings from the Royal Collection. To her and to the many other lenders the Trustees and I express our warmest gratitude; without their wholehearted enthusiasm and cooperation there would be no Van Dyck exhibition for the public to enjoy. The response has been so remarkable, indeed, that there are few gaps in Sir Oliver's original list. Perhaps the saddest loss is the moving double portrait in the Prado in which Van Dyck contrasts his own appearance, elegant but, as always, tense, looking backwards over his shoulder at the spectator, with that of his bluff and jovial friend, Endymion Porter.

JOHN HAYES
Director, National Portrait Gallery
August 1982

Acknowledgements

I am grateful, once more, to Dr John Hayes for the invitation to organize an exhibition in the National Portrait Gallery. The portraits which Van Dyck painted in England when he was in the service of Charles I are the most distinguished and splendid ever painted in this country, and they exercised an incalculable influence on the future course of British portrait painting. It is appropriate that the first large exhibition to be devoted solely to the painter's English period should be held at the National Portrait Gallery.

The generosity of owners and the co-operation of curators have enabled us to assemble an impressive range of pictures and drawings. Certain very large paintings could not be expected to be allowed to make the journey from abroad; and the serious student will have to make an excursion to Wilton to see a huge and immovable masterpiece in a celebrated setting. One or two very important portraits in the United States, which came to the Tate Gallery ten years ago, were not released on this occasion, but owners in the British Isles have responded with characteristic generosity to our requests. We had only two refusals, but they left irreplaceable gaps in the exhibition as we at first envisaged it. Neither the full-length of the patron who wrote a eulogistic letter to the painter nor Van Dyck's finest double portrait was allowed by its owner to come to the exhibition.

Nevertheless, the pictures assembled make, we trust, a noble display, and they include a number of portraits which will not be familiar to any but the specialist. The exhibition will, I hope, stimulate fresh speculation on some of the problems presented by Van Dyck's work in this country: the organization of his practice, for example, his methods and techniques, the chronology of his English portraits and the changes, which do not seem to follow automatically a straightforward course, in his style in the English years. More important, perhaps, is the pleasure to be derived from seeing these beautiful and imaginative works of art and from assessing their significance for the taste and ideals of the court of Charles I as well as for the future of British painting.

In working on the exhibition I have become especially conscious that I have not seen some of the portraits for many years. Essential comparisons have not, therefore, always been possible, and even conscientious note-taking cannot ensure that impressions remain valid or even worthwhile. I hope that the suggestions and judgements put forward will not seem invariably too far-fetched or subjective.

I am very grateful to Mr Christopher Brown, Professor Michael Jaffé and Mr Gregory Martin for many conversations and discussions on Van Dyck, not necessarily in connection with this exhibition. Once again, it has been a great pleasure to work with Dr Malcolm Rogers and to experience once more his enthusiasm and courtesy. I have benefited greatly from talking about Van Dyck's technique with Miss Viola Pemberton-Pigott, Miss Amelia Jackson and Mr Herbert Lank and his colleagues at the Hamilton Kerr Institute and in Ebury Street. I am again much indebted to Miss Jacquie Meredith, Miss Honor Clerk and Miss Mary Pettman for their work in assembling the exhibits and preparing the catalogue. It is, as always, a great pleasure to have worked with Mr Graham Johnson and Mr Joe Pradera over the design of the catalogue and the exhibition respectively. Other debts I hope to have acknowledged in the appropriate places, but I would especially like to thank Dr Aileen Ribeiro of the History of Dress Department at the Courtauld Institute for a conversation on dress in Van Dyck's portraits; Miss Alison Pennie for translating two passages from the Russian catalogue of the Van Dycks in The Hermitage; and Miss Caroline Crichton-Stuart for her care in preparing a difficult manuscript for the press.

O.N.M.
July 1982

Wenceslaus Hollar, after Van Dyck, *Portrait of the Artist*

Introduction

The years spent by Anthony van Dyck in London, in the service of Charles I, are the most dramatic in the history of English painting. When he arrived in London in the early spring of 1632, he was one of the most successful and accomplished painters in Europe. He had been trained in the largest and most efficiently organized studio on the Continent and had spent a number of years in Italy. Distinguished in appearance, accustomed to moving in the grandest circles, he was perfectly equipped to work at the early Stuart court, where his knowledge of contemporary European painting and his particular devotion to the memory of Titian would have made him a valuable friend and adviser to the *cognoscenti* of the 'Whitehall group', and would especially have endeared him to the King. Charles I had wanted for many years to attract to his service a painter of international reputation and he found in Van Dyck a painter who shared many of his own tastes and especially his love of Titian. Outwardly at least there has never been a more civilized court in this country than the one presided over by Charles I and his Queen; and Van Dyck's portraits are the most refined, evocative and influential works of art created in that glamorous setting. The illusion the portraits had helped to sustain collapsed at the approach of civil war and discord, so often personified by artists and writers as the antithesis of peace under whose benign and fruitful influence the arts could flourish. On the development of painting in this country the work of Van Dyck at the court of Charles I, during the years of the King's absolute rule, wrought a revolution as dramatic in its way as any other upheaval in that turbulent age.

James I had been passionately attached to the cause of peace; and in the early years of his reign, when the storms of war had begun to subside on the Continent, an interest in the arts began to develop surprisingly rapidly at the English court among a group of collectors and connoisseurs, a number of whom were associated with the young Prince of Wales, the elder brother of the future. Charles I. Travel on the Continent was becoming easier and contacts were established between England and the Continent in the artistic field, principally by the King's ambassadors or special envoys. Collectors at home were able to employ agents to scour Europe for classical, Renaissance and contemporary works of art or to invite foreign artists and craftsmen to try their fortunes in London. The part played by diplomats in bringing the arts of the Continent to this country can hardly be over-estimated; and the effect of this new and expansive phase in the history of English taste was to set this country for the first time since the Reformation completely within the orbit of the Continent.

Antwerp, in the early years of the century, was gradually recovering something of its former prosperity after the ravages of the siege by the Duke of Parma. The Southern Netherlands had returned to their ancient allegiance and were once again irrevocably united with Spain: firmly under a Spanish administration and subjected to the full force of a revived Catholic Church fired with the spirit of the Counter-Reformation and determined to revitalize the religious life of the province. The Catholic revival in the South was an essential part of a general renaissance in learning and the arts which was coloured by ancient Burgundian tradition and steeped in classical antiquity and the Italian Renaissance. To the art-historian this activity is illuminated with special brilliance in the life and work of Rubens, who had returned to Antwerp at the end of 1608. Within a few months of his return the Twelve Years Truce was concluded with the Dutch.

English travellers and envoys, on the look-out for works of art for collectors at home, were impressed by what they saw in the studios of the Antwerp painters. Inevitably there was a particular interest in Rubens and his work. In the summer of 1620 a particularly grand traveller, the Countess of Arundel, was passing through Antwerp on her way to Italy. Rubens had been asked by the Earl to paint a portrait of her. He claimed that he had turned down commissions from many princes and gentlemen, but he could not refuse a patron whom he described as one of the four evangelists and supporters of his art. In a letter to the Earl about the progress of the portrait the earliest notice of Van Dyck in an English context is to be found. Arundel's Venetian *gentiluomo*, Francesco Vercellini, acting as the Countess's factotum on her travels, wrote to Arundel on 17 July 1620 about the progress of the picture. He described Rubens's method in putting together so large and complex a composition – a method which Van Dyck must often have observed and was himself to imitate – and added a note about Rubens's young associate: 'Van Dyck is still with Rubens and his works are coming to be scarcely less highly esteemed than those of his master; he is a young man of twenty-one, and his father and mother, who are very rich, live in this city; so that it will be difficult for him to leave these parts, all the more as he sees the good fortune that attends Rubens'.[1]

The young man in whom Arundel had shown an interest, of whose abilities he could have heard from a number of possible contacts in Flanders, and whom he was presumably hoping to persuade to come to London, had been born in Antwerp on 22 March 1599, the seventh child of Frans van Dyck, a merchant trading in silk, linen and other materials, and also President of the Confraternity of the Holy Sacrament in Antwerp Cathedral. His mother, Maria Cuperis or Cuypers, was famous for her skill as an embroiderer. As a boy Van Dyck had been apprenticed to Hendrick van Balen, and at the age of ten had been enrolled as Van Balen's pupil in the Guild of St Luke in Antwerp. Van Balen's influence on him is hard to detect; by the time he was registered as a master in the records of the Guild in February 1618 Van Dyck had been established in his own studio for a few years and had two young assistants working with him. He had fallen inevitably under the influence of Rubens, who referred to him in April 1618 as 'the best of my pupils'. He had painted one of the pictures mentioned in a list of works in Rubens's house – 'the flower of my stock' – which were being offered to Sir Dudley Carleton, who was ambassador to The Hague and very active on behalf of collectors in England.[2] Although Vercellini had at first been doubtful whether Van Dyck could be persuaded to travel to London, Carleton was informed in a postscript to a letter written on 25 November 1620 by Toby Matthew in Antwerp that 'Van Dike his [ie Rubens's] famous Allievo is gone into England, and y^t the Kinge hath given him a Pension of £100 p^r ann'.[3]

Toby Matthew's postscript is not easy to interpret, but it seems that Van Dyck had taken with him the 'desseigne' of a *Hunt of Lions and Tigers* which Rubens – 'ye cruell courteous Paynter' – was anxious to sell, through Carleton, to Lord Danvers who wished to give it to the Prince of Wales. The *Hunt* was, however, severely criticized by the painters in London as a picture scarcely touched by Rubens himself, and the Prince (soon to be described by Rubens as the greatest lover of pictures in the world) refused to admit it into his gallery in St James's Palace. The young Van Dyck

Fig.1 *Portrait of a Man*. Collection of the Prince of Liechtenstein, Vaduz

Fig.2 *Portrait of a Man*. Gemäldegalerie, Dresden

found himself, therefore, at the heart of a dispute among painters, connoisseurs and their agents at Whitehall. This was the stage on which he was to play so prominent a part in due course; Lord Danvers, indeed, was to be the subject of one of his most distinguished works (no.20).[4]

Matthew considered that the young man would paint a much better picture in London than the second-rate *Hunt*, and for half the price. Very little is known of what Van Dyck did on this first visit to London, but he painted at least one picture for each of the principal collectors at the Jacobean court. For the Marquess of Buckingham (as he then was) he painted the *Continence of Scipio* (no.3). The Earl of Arundel sat to him for his portrait (no.2). In the galleries of these two Jacobean connoisseurs Van Dyck would have seen works by the Venetian painters who had already begun to exercise an influence on him at home. As a painter he was outstandingly precocious, perceptive, ambitious and technically brilliantly gifted. He could also absorb with an almost dangerous facility any new artistic influence or idea that appealed to him; he had charming manners and a distinguished appearance; and he could adapt himself with ease to a new environment, however grand. His early portraits (eg fig.1) had been recognizably in the tradition of Pourbus (the elder and younger), Coello or Adriaen Key. The sitters stand in sober costume, motionless against a plain background. Van Dyck remained attached longer than Rubens had done to an old-fashioned tradition that had developed originally from Anthonis Mor. His earliest portraits are basically very close to Rubens; their technical virtuosity does not always conceal some structural weakness and they are often tinged with an underlying melancholy, an indefinably reticent and introspective mood which sets them apart from the confidence that always pervades a portrait by Rubens.

Fig.3 *Family Group*. The Hermitage, Leningrad

Fig.4 Titian, *Jacopo Strada*. Kunsthistorisches Museum, Vienna

Before he left Antwerp Van Dyck's portraits had become more relaxed. The plain backgrounds are replaced by a glimpse of sky and landscape beyond a curtain or a column and the sitters begin to move with less constraint in a more natural atmosphere. The first sign of this comes in a portrait in Dresden (fig.2), where a gentleman pulls on a glove. These developments in his style were stimulated mainly by his increasing interest in the great Venetian painters of the previous century. The influence of Tintoretto, Veronese, Jacopo Bassano and, above all, Titian permeates the work of Van Dyck from now on. His sense of colour, his handling and his choice of accessories and dress reflect the admiration he felt for the Venetian portrait-patterns with their exciting movement and gesture; but above all for the ease and unstated authority, the combination of grandeur and relaxation, that 'certaine mooving vertue', which he found again and again in the work of Titian and in his own work so often reinterprets in contemporary terms. In the early family groups (eg fig.3) or the portrait of George Gage (no.1) the understanding of character and the sense of movement would be difficult to find in the work of an earlier Flemish painter and in part reflect Venetian influence. The subject-matter in the portrait of Gage, and the dramatic diagonals in the composition, may have been inspired by a picture such as Titian's *Jacopo Strada* (fig.4).

The portrait of Arundel is painted on canvas, which Van Dyck increasingly used in preference to panel as a support; the paint is rough, thin and dry, unlike the richly impasted pigment of his earlier portraits; and the figure sits with an appropriate air of grandeur against the background of curtain and sky. In the picture painted for Buckingham (no.3) the influence of Rubens is distilled in a highly idiosyncratic way, influenced, above all, by Veronese, in whose works this patron's collection was

Fig.5 Veronese, *Esther and Ahasuerus*. Kunsthistorisches Museum, Vienna

Fig.6 *Samson and Delilah*. Dulwich Picture Gallery

particularly rich (eg fig.5). The influence of such a painter – and of a new environment – worked with enormous speed on a painter who had, only a few months
earlier, been painting in Antwerp pictures which had been structurally and technically very close to Rubens although they too were charged with an individual spirit
and had been designed on the same narrow stage (eg fig.6).[5] The fundamental
distinction between the two artists was that Rubens's interest in sculpture enabled
him to design forms and compositions in the round, whereas Van Dyck always
thought in terms of line and surface.

Fig. 7 *Jupiter and Ceres* (?). Palazzo Bianco, Genoa

On 16 February 1621 an order was made for payment to Van Dyck of £100 as reward for 'speciall service' performed by him for the King.[6] Nothing is known of the work Van Dyck had done for James I. It is possible (see no.66) that he painted a portrait of him. It is also conceivable that the King hoped to employ him at his newly established tapestry factory at Mortlake. At least one much less distinguished Flemish artist, Abraham van Blyenberch, was working at this period on designs for tapestries to be woven at Mortlake; and Van Dyck's sense of linear design and his experience of designing for tapestry in Rubens's studio would have fitted him perfectly for such a task (*The Continence of Scipio* would be admirably suited for a tapestry). However, on 28 February, a fortnight after receiving the payment from the King, Van Dyck was granted, as His Majesty's servant, a pass to travel for eight months, 'As was sygnifyed by the E of Arundell'.[7] He went to Antwerp and, in the autumn, set off for Italy. That year the Twelve Years Truce expired and the war between north and south in the Netherlands was resumed.

Van Dyck probably remained in Italy until the autumn of 1627. By 1628 he had re-established his studio in Antwerp and he did not return to London until the spring of 1632. In Italy he seems to have passed beyond the ken of his former English patrons. Little, indeed, was known in England of the pictures he painted in Italy until the early years of the nineteenth century. He travelled as far as Sicily and visited, or worked in, Florence, Rome, Bologna, Venice, Mantua, Milan and Turin; but the greater part of his time was spent in Genoa. In Italy he used the famous *Sketchbook* for notes of pictures which he particularly admired; among them Titian's work predominates. While he was in Italy his style expanded dramatically. In at least one huge altarpiece he reinterpreted an early baroque masterpiece by Rubens;

Fig.8 *Anton Giulio Brignole Sale*. Palazzo Rosso, Genoa

Fig.9 *The Lomellini Family*. National Gallery of Scotland, Edinburgh

but in his mythological subjects (eg fig.7) he produced a pastiche of Titian which foreshadows in its curious twilight mood the last stage of his work in this genre. In his portraits he developed the full repertory of his later years. He painted at least two large equestrian portraits (eg fig.8), one very big full-length family group (fig.9) and a succession of noble full-lengths (eg fig.10), in which there is an obvious debt to the full-lengths by Rubens which he would have found in Genoa (eg *Brigida Spinola Doria*(?) at Kingston Lacy). He had painted a few full-lengths in Antwerp, but on these great canvases Van Dyck captured the atmosphere of the sombre Genoese *palazzi* in which his patrons lived, and set them with supreme distinction against backgrounds of columns and curtains which are superbly deployed. His paint at this period is drier and generally thinner than it had been earlier and the tonality dark, rich and sparkling. The portraits reveal a wide range of sympathy and observation. An ancient senator, a beautiful marchesa or her enchanting children are portrayed with equal understanding. His exceptional ability as a painter of children is first seen in this period. Van Dyck's Italian portraits are often painted on a bigger scale than hitherto and they display above all a new and dramatic sense of movement (eg fig.11). In the masterpiece of the earlier Italian period (fig.12) there is a play of subtle movement in the figure and the whole composition is alive as if stirred by a sudden draught through the cool corridors of a Roman palace. Some of his Italian sitters move across the canvas, casting a glance behind them as they go.

In Italy his success in the highest social circles and the glamour of the environment in which he worked turned him into a finished courtier-artist. There is a good deal of well-merited self-satisfaction in the image of himself (fig.13) which he had probably painted (in at least three versions) on the eve of his departure for Italy. In Italy, according to Bellori's vivid description, he cut a distinguished figure. Although he was small, he affected the manners of a nobleman. He sported a little beard and wore grand clothes, a feathered hat and a gold chain. He was attended by

Fig.10 *Marchesa Brignole Sale and her Son.* National Gallery of Art, Washington

Fig.11 *Lucas van Uffelen.* Metropolitan Museum of Art, New York

Fig.12 *Cardinal Bentivoglio.* Galleria Pitti, Florence

Fig.13 *Self-portrait.* The Hermitage, Leningrad

Colour plate I Teresia, Lady Shirley (no.5) c 1622

Colour plate II François Langlois (no. 10) c. 1634

Colour plate III William Laud, Archbishop of Canterbury (no.14)

Colour plate IV William Feilding, 1st Earl of Denbigh (no. 16) c 1633

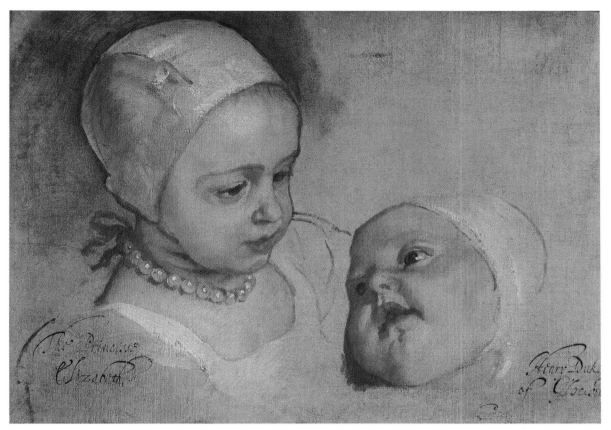

Colour plate v Princess Elizabeth and Princess Anne (no.27)

Colour plate VI *Detail from* Dorothy, Viscountess Andover, and her sister Elizabeth, Lady Thimbleby (no.29)

The Countes of Cleueland wife to
Tho: wentworth Earl of Cleueland

Colour plate VII Anne Crofts, Countess of Cleveland (no.31)

Colour plate VIII Thomas Killigrew (no.39)   1638

Colour plate IX   Lord John Stuart with his brother, Lord Bernard Stuart, later Earl of Lichfield
(no.44)

c. 1639

Colour plate x Queen Henrietta Maria (no.53)

c1638

Colour plate XI Thomas Wentworth, Earl of Strafford, with Sir Philip Mainwaring (no.57)

Colour plate XII William II, Prince of Orange, with Mary, Princess Royal (no.62)

c1641

a train of servants.[8] The example of Rubens must have been always in his mind; even the decision to go to Italy must have owed much to Rubens's influence, and at the court of James I conversation must continually have been about Rubens. By now, however, Van Dyck had developed into an artist of a very different sort. He did not have Rubens's magnificent mental and physical stamina or his organizing ability; Van Dyck could never have overseen a large studio in which to produce big decorative schemes or large cycles of paintings. He did not share Rubens's intellectual interests or understanding of architecture and sculpture. As De Piles said, 'his Mind was not of so large an extent, as that of *Ruben's*'. He had nothing of Rubens's enthusiasm for archaeology or classical history and classical literature; there is nothing in Van Dyck's *œuvre*, for example, to compare with Rubens's title-pages. Nor was he attracted by the glamour of the Burgundian past or the picturesque possibilities of fifteenth-century Flemish costume. Pageantry, daemonic or apocalyptic visions, Bacchic scenes, hunts and other savage subjects had little appeal for him. Even by the end of the Italian period the proportion of portraits to his works in other genres was far higher than it was in Rubens's *œuvre*; and it was on his portraits that his reputation and influence were chiefly to rest and to endure.

When he came back from Italy to Flanders Van Dyck embarked on a period of intense activity and notable success: a period in which he produced his finest work as painter of religious and mythological subjects as well as portraits, and in which he resumed his contacts with the English court. Rubens, moreover, was away from Antwerp between September 1628 and March 1630. By May 1630 Van Dyck was described as painter to the Regent, the widowed Archduchess Isabella. He had painted a successful portrait of her (very closely related to an earlier image by Rubens) soon after his arrival in Antwerp and was rewarded with a chain of gold valued at 750 florins.[9] He was unquestionably the leading portrait painter in the Southern Netherlands; and he was continuously employed by the Church. He painted large altarpieces in the full Counter-Reformation style. For more intimate settings in private houses or chapels he painted smaller devotional pictures in a neo-Venetian manner which he had begun to develop in Italy. His religious pieces are refined in quality and have a tender and very personal charm (eg fig.14). It is significant that they were to exercise a considerable influence on Spanish painting; and the religious pictures which Van Dyck is reported by Bellori to have painted in England would have been in this vein. In December 1631 Balthazar Gerbier had bought for the Earl of Portland, as a New Year's gift to the King and Queen, '*une fort belle Notre Dame et Ste. Catherine faict de la main de Van Dyck*' which the Archduchess had placed in the private chapel used by Marie de' Medici, Queen Henrietta Maria's mother, in Brussels.[10] The mythological subjects of this period are equally sophisticated. On 23 March 1630 Endymion Porter, whom Van Dyck had met in London on his brief visit ten years earlier and who had been in touch with him once more in Antwerp, received from Charles I seventy-eight pounds for 'one picture of the Storie of Reynaldo & Armida' which the King had commissioned from Van Dyck.[11] This is thought to be the picture in Baltimore (fig.15), the finest of Van Dyck's mature mythological compositions. It is not difficult to imagine the delight with which this beautiful picture, with its Venetian harmonies, fluttering movement, linear rhythms and sensuous pigment, its refined characterization and form, would have been received in London. The influence of Rubens is now imperceptible. In such a picture

Van Dyck is constructing the stylistic link between the Venetian painters of the previous century and Boucher.

Before he came over to England Van Dyck paid two visits to The Hague, where he painted portraits of the Prince and Princess of Orange and of their son, who was eventually to marry the English Princess Royal and to figure in Van Dyck's last important royal commission (no.62).[12] The portraits painted in his second Flemish period are the most consistently distinguished and accomplished, in design and in technique, that he ever painted. Particularly sympathetic are those of fellow-artists and members of their families (eg fig.16). Two fine examples were already in Charles I's possession and one (no.6) was traditionally said to have impressed the King so much that he 'gave order' for the artist to be 'sent for over into England'. The full-lengths of the King's young nephews, Charles Louis and Rupert, painted in Holland on the eve of the artist's journey to London, epitomize his achievement so far. The splendour of the Genoese full-lengths is combined with a new mastery of design. In the portrait of the younger boy (fig.17) a subtle play of twists and thrusts down the figure is stabilized by the column and ledge which support him. The simple black silhouette is relieved by the gold of the chain and the hilt of the sword and is set off by the silver-grey in the architecture and the beautiful greens in the curtain and the landscape. The quality of paint is wonderfully fresh throughout. As a court portrait, such an image was, within its own terms, unsurpassed in Europe at this time.[13]

By 1 April 1632 Van Dyck was in London. Gerbier, in his correspondence with the Earl of Portland about his present for the King and Queen, had reported from Brussels on 13 March that Van Dyck, who had resolved to go to England, apparently on behalf of Marie de' Medici and the Archduchess and *avecq leurs portraits*', had suddenly decided to abandon the idea. His characteristic capriciousness had offended the Archduchess. He had tried to discredit the picture which Gerbier had secured and was using 'that babbler' Geldorp to discredit Gerbier as well. Rubens who, as Gerbier said, was *le maistre en ce Pays*', remarked that Van Dyck would have to be put to the test, when he arrived in England, to see if he could do better. By 1 April, however, he was in London, bringing with him portraits of the Prince and Princess of Orange and their son, the Archduchess and Henrietta Maria's younger brother, the Duke of Orléans, who had taken refuge in Brussels with his mother after the fiasco of the Day of Dupes. These portraits were among those for which Van Dyck was to be paid in August.[14]

At first Van Dyck 'and his servants' were lodged, at the King's expense, with Edward Norgate, best known as the writer of a treatise on miniature painting. The King said that Inigo Jones was to be consulted about a house for Van Dyck and in due course he took up residence at Blackfriars, in the parish of St Anne's, where his rent was paid by the Crown. In 1634 his establishment included six servants who were listed among the 128 'Dutchmen' who lived in the Precinct of Blackfriars. One of these 'Dutchmen', 'Iasper Lanfranck', died in February 1639; another servant, 'Martin Ashent', described as Van Dyck's man, died a month later. The house was on the waterside and had a garden. A new causeway and stairs were constructed so that, in the months of June and July 1635, the King could go down by water to see Van Dyck's paintings.[15] In the summer Van Dyck made use of a residence at Eltham, presumably in the King's House in Eltham Palace. Here, in the summer of

Fig.14 *Rest on the Flight into Egypt*. Alte Pinakothek, Munich

Fig.15 *Rinaldo and Armida*. Museum of Art, Baltimore

Fig.16 *Mme de Nole and her Daughter*. Alte Pinakothek, Munich

Fig.17 *Prince Rupert*. Kunsthistorisches Museum, Vienna

1636, when the plague was rife in London, Strafford (see no.23) sat to Van Dyck; and here Vertue saw, many years later, monochrome sketches of scenes from Ovid, painted on panels in the house in which, by tradition, Van Dyck had spent 'the Summer season'.[16]

On 5 July 1632 Van Dyck, described as 'Principal Painter in Ordinary to their Majesties', was knighted at St James's and on 17 October 1633 was granted an annuity or yearly pension of £200 to run from the previous March.[17] Both Daniel Mytens and Cornelius Johnson, who had earlier been appointed 'picture-drawers of our chamber in ordinary', were still in the King's service, but the last payments to Mytens were made in 1634 and Johnson, once Van Dyck was established, was seldom to be seen near the court. Van Dyck was henceforth to have a virtual monopoly in portraits of the King and Queen 'in large', but on a painter of his increasingly neurotic temperament and frail physique the strains imposed by his position and duties must have been considerable. He would be responsible for producing royal portraits for despatch overseas and for presentation at home, although Charles I, who had retained no full-length portraits of himself – or the Queen – by any of Van Dyck's predecessors, kept for his own use many of Van Dyck's most important presentations of 'Our Royall self and most dearest Consort the Queene'. Early in May 1633 there were nine pictures of the King and Queen for which Van Dyck was due for payment (£444); and records of royal payments survive from 21 October 1633 (£40 for a portrait of the Queen for Wentworth); 23 February 1637 (when £1200 was due to him for 'certain pictures' for the King's use); and 25 February 1639 (£305 for 'certain pictures' provided for the King). The price of the pictures, in the 'Memoire', amounted, with the arrears of his pension which for five years had remained unpaid, to £1603, and the sum due for the pictures (£603) was apparently paid in two instalments in the winter of 1638–9.[18] His work at court would have involved such dreary chores as painting posthumous portraits with which the Queen could complete a historical portrait gallery at Somerset House. He was prepared to undertake such commissions for favoured patrons like Northumberland and Pembroke, but even from the King and Queen he refused a commission to paint them together at length in a perspective background painted by Steenwyck.

Such journeyman work would have come more easily to Van Dyck's predecessors whose work, even at its most sympathetic and accomplished, he was to render old-fashioned within months of his arrival. In a series of large compositions painted to be strategically placed at different points in the King's various 'houses of resort', the power and splendour of the British monarchy and the early Stuart dynasty were displayed with an imaginative power and a technical brilliance which had never been seen before in this country and on a scale which only a painter of Van Dyck's ability and experience could manage. The original impact of these huge compositions must have been considerable. Much of Van Dyck's work relies for its effect on illusion; technique, imagination and sympathy are combined to create the impression that these great designs are wholly original. In fact Van Dyck drew on a wide variety of sources with which to bring up to date iconographical themes originally worked out for the Tudors. In his first large royal group, the 'Great Piece' of 1632 (no.7), he remodels on a big scale, in modern terms and with rare charm, a composition which had first been designed for Henry VIII. The huge equestrian portrait of Charles I (no.11), a subtle tribute to the King as ruler and patron, is also

the last and grandest variation on a Renaissance theme which had been developed by Rubens and exploited in the Antwerp studios in Van Dyck's youth. The later equestrian portrait, now in the National Gallery, takes the traditional figure of the King as a warrior, the archetypal iconographical pattern which is to be seen on the obverse of the Great Seal, in engravings of a number of distinguished figures in the Elizabethan and Jacobean periods, and in at least one portrait on the scale of life of the King's famous elder brother; and sets it, on a heroic scale, in a twilit sylvan setting.[19] The most romantic of all Van Dyck's presentations of the King is the portrait '*à la chasse*' in the Louvre (fig.18). The synthesis of earlier variations on the theme of a royal figure in the hunting-field with elements taken from Titian, or from Titian through Rubens, creates a quintessential image of unstressed royal authority and, for posterity, the archetypal picture of the 'brave prince of cavaliers'. As a design it shows Van Dyck developing a theme with a sophistication which no other painter in royal service could emulate. It is not clear exactly when Mytens produced his big canvas of Charles I and Henrietta Maria setting off for the chase (fig.19), but it is not impossible that it was painted just after Van Dyck's arrival in London; and '*Le Roi à la Chasse*', and the full-length of Henrietta Maria dressed for the chase (fig.20), can to some extent be taken together as examples of the ease with which he could take over and transfigure a predecessor's pedestrian efforts.[20]

To Bellori the most significant influence in Van Dyck's second equestrian portrait of Charles I was Titian's portrait of Charles V at the battle of Muhlberg. Van Dyck, he considered, had painted the King '*à cavallo ad imitatione di Carlo Quinto espresso da Titiano*'; and he regarded him, in some of his portraits, as '*con l'istesso Titiano maraviglioso*'.[21] One English contemporary wrote of him that 'he emulated Titian,

Fig.19 Daniel Mytens, *Charles I and Henrietta Maria with Jeffery Hudson.* Hampton Court (reproduced by gracious permission of Her Majesty The Queen)

Fig.20 *Henrietta Maria with Jeffery Hudson.* National Gallery of Art, Washington

whom Charles V translated to the ranks of the nobility; so our Charles appointed this follower of Titian to the order of the Golden Knights'.[22] He was considered to know so much about Titian's technique that the King, before Van Dyck came to London, had sent two of the *Roman Emperors*, which had arrived from Mantua badly damaged, to Brussels to be restored. The first payments made by the King to Van Dyck, on 8 August 1632, included £5 for 'mending' *Galba* and £20 for a new picture of *Vitellius*. The original had been 'utterlie spoyled . . . and quite washed away'.[23]

Towards the end of his career Van Dyck charged £50 to £60 for a standard full-length, £30 for a half-length and £20 for a head-and-shoulders portrait. A full-length by Daniel Mytens, by the end of his time in England, could cost a patron £50 if it contained such extras as regalia, or a 'prospect'. Normal full-lengths from Mytens's early years in England had cost £30; but his full-length of the Queen with Jeffery Hudson cost as much as £80. On the other hand Mytens only received an annual salary of £70. For bigger pictures, such as the King '*à la chasse*' or the group of his eldest children (no.26), Van Dyck hoped to receive £200. After the King's execution the equestrian portrait from St James's (no.11) was valued at £150; the picture now in the National Gallery was valued at £200. A double portrait (such as no.30) was valued at £40, but made £50 when it was sold. *Cupid and Psyche* (no.58) was sold in 1651 for £110. Prices of copies produced in the studio may have varied. Strafford, a hard man to bargain with, considered £20 and £30 fair prices for copies (which we should perhaps have described as replicas) of half-lengths and full-lengths respectively, especially if a lot were being ordered at one time.

Van Dyck lived in considerable style. He earned a lot of money, but must have spent it freely in keeping up an establishment in which he could entertain his grand clients. Margaret Lemon (no.80) does not sound the kind of companion to be content, while she was under his roof, with the proverbial dinner of herbs. Van Dyck

Fig.21 Daniel Mytens, *Henry Rich, 1st Earl of Holland.*
National Portrait Gallery, London

Fig.22 *Robert Rich, 2nd Earl of Warwick.* Metropolitan
Museum of Art, New York

also spent a lot of money on pictures. A fine collection included, according to his
inventory, nineteen Titians. Among them were *Perseus and Andromeda*, now in the
Wallace Collection, and the *Vendramin Family* in the National Gallery, both of which
were secured after the painter's death by the Earl of Northumberland, and the
Portrait of a Man, formerly called Ariosto, in the National Gallery, which he may have
been encouraged to acquire at the end of his life by François Langlois (no.10).[24]
When Marie de' Medici had sat to Van Dyck in Antwerp, her secretary had admired
his collection of Titians and compared his fame with Titian's; and in England the
impact of the many works by Titian which he saw intensified the effect of his
influence upon him.

With his distinguished appearance, cultivated manners and wide experience, Van
Dyck could obviously be charming company. The Marquess of Newcastle was as
enchanted with the painter as with the portraits he had painted for him: 'The favors
off my freindes you have so transmitted unto mee as the longer I Looke on them, the
more I thinke them Nature & nott Arte'. His judgement might, he feared, be
defective, but his admiration was unbounded; and he could claim 'the Luck to be
astonish'de In the righte Place'. It was perhaps during sittings for his own portrait
that he had enjoyed 'the Blessinge off your Companye, & Sweetnes off Conversation'.[25] It is unlikely that any of Van Dyck's predecessors at the early Stuart court
would have provided a patron with such a pleasant experience; nor was any other

23

Fig.23 Daniel Mytens, *Algernon Percy, 10th Earl of Northumberland*. Viscount De L'Isle

Fig.24 Artist unknown, *William Feilding, 1st Earl of Denbigh*. Whereabouts unknown

painter of the day eulogized in verse by Waller, Cowley and Herrick.

It was not only his fine collection, lavish way of life and cosmopolitan manner that made the other painters in London look antiquated. Van Dyck transformed, within a short time of his arrival, the way in which sitters would see themselves on a canvas. The portraits he painted at the English court are nearer in feeling and design to Gainsborough than to Mytens. Almost invariably, in portraits by Mytens, for example, or Cornelius Johnson, the figure looks straight out at the spectator and the whole length of the figure is set at an unvarying angle to the surface of the picture. Nor, within the figure, is there any movement or gesture to disturb this formal pattern. Perhaps only in one composition (fig.21) does Mytens, probably under the influence of Van Dyck, make his sitter look away from the spectator and at least think about moving across the surface of the canvas: against, incidentally, a land-scape backcloth almost unprecedented in his work. In Van Dyck's masterly portrait of Lord Denbigh (no.16), the sitter steps forward through the landscape; and in the superbly authoritative portrait of the Earl of Warwick (fig.22) the sitter moves with a swinging stride across the canvas in a way that foreshadows an early masterpiece by Reynolds. In both portraits the turn of the head sets off a dramatic counterpoise to the main thrust of the figure. It is a revelation to compare a portrait by Van Dyck with a portrait of the same sitter by a more pedestrian painter, trained in the Dutch manner. The transformation of the King himself at the hands of his chosen painter has often been analysed; but all Van Dyck's sitters are transfigured. His *Earl of Northumberland* (eg no.24), for instance, or *Sir Thomas Hanmer* are not recognizable as the subjects of quiet likenesses by Mytens (fig.23) or Johnson; and the comparison

Fig.25 William Larkin (?), *Anne Countess of Stamford*. Ranger's House, Blackheath (GLC)

Fig.26 *Anne, Countess of Clanbrassil*. Copyright the Frick Collection, New York

between a slightly earlier full-length of Denbigh (fig.24) with Van Dyck's portrait re-emphasizes Van Dyck's significance for the painters of the eighteenth century. Van Dyck's sophisticated technique, moreover, can bring to life the whole surface – costume, accessories and background – with a lively, flickering, nervous touch. A shimmering sense of movement and a swift interchange of glance would have enlivened a gallery of portraits, 'where glittering courtiers in their tissues stalk'd',[26] fresh from his 'shop of beauty': in Northumberland House, in Lord Wharton's gallery or in the house of Lady Hatton where Richard Symonds saw six ladies' portraits at length, 'a little Country or a Table & carpet by y^m'.[27] The sitters in a Jacobean long gallery, with their rigid stance, unblinking gaze and polished accessories and dress (eg fig.25), would seem to be occupying another world; Van Dyck's *Lady Clanbrassil* (fig.26) inhabits the same world (she used, indeed, to inhabit the same room in the Frick Collection) as Gainsborough's *Mrs Baker* (fig.27) and *Frances Duncombe*.

Van Dyck's influence in breaking the rigid moulds within which his older contemporaries had cast their sitters was almost immediate. Adriaen Hanneman was quickly influenced by Van Dyck's technique and repertory. One or two of Cornelius Johnson's sitters turn their heads away, his draperies become more *mouvementé* and a hand is occasionally introduced into the design of his smaller portraits. The sitters in

Fig.27 Thomas Gainsborough, *Mrs Baker*. Copyright the Frick Collection, New York

Fig.28 Cornelius Johnson, *Frances, Marchioness of Hertford* (1633). Petworth

his full-lengths abandon their former stiff posture (eg fig.28) and advance uncertainly across the composition (eg fig.29). His treatment of backgrounds and drapery becomes recognizably Van Dyckian in intention. Van Dyck's manner was passing into the mainstream of British painting; and it is a fruitful exercise to identify the sources from which he created the range of designs which together formed a thematic pattern-book for his successors, and to see how they plagiarized or reinterpreted them. On the Continent, too, his work was soon to exercise a profound influence on the development of late baroque and early rococo portrait painting; but none of his successors attained the supreme distinction, reticence and refinement which made him so aristocratic an artist.

It would be a simplification to say that Van Dyck flattered his sitters. The Countess of Sussex (who was subsequently to be married to the Earl of Warwick) had reluctantly agreed to sit to Van Dyck in the winter of 1639–40, though she thought the money 'ill bestowde'. Although the painter was prevailed upon to fine down her cheeks a little, the Countess was distressed when she saw the finished portrait. She thought it 'very ill favourede, makes me quite out of love with myselfe, the face is so bige and so fate that it pleses me not att all. It lokes lyke on of the windes poffinge – but truly I thinke it tis lyke the originale'. She intended, if she came to London before Van Dyck departed, to ask him to 'mende' the portrait, 'for thow I bee ill favourede i think that makes me wors than I am'.[28] Against this must be set the reaction of the young Princess Sophia, Prince Rupert's youngest sister, when she saw the Queen for the first time. Her ideas on the beauty of all English ladies had been

Fig.29 Cornelius Johnson, *Mary Coventry* (1641). The Marquess of Bath

Fig.30 *George, Lord Digby, and William, Lord Russell.* The Earl Spencer

derived from 'the fine portraits of Van Dyck'; so it was a surprise to find the Queen '(so beautiful in her picture) a little woman with long lean arms, crooked shoulders, and teeth protruding from her mouth like guns from a fort'.[29] In his most profound study of the King (no.22) Van Dyck provides a revealing contrast between the coarsely moulded features of the profile and the remote and sensitive frontal image that gazes out at us. Van Dyck's natural tendency was to refine the features of a sitter, to emphasize the distinguished qualities in a face, or subtly to enhance a sitter's appearance rather as Lawrence was to do. If, for example, the coarse features and fleshy hands of Mytens's 4th Earl of Pembroke (fig.37) are compared with Van Dyck's treatment of them (no.12), the refining process, the emphasis on bone and tendon, can be seen subtly to ennoble, almost to etherealize, the sitter. 'He took his Time', in the words of De Piles, 'to draw a Face when it had its best looks on'; he heightened nature 'as far as he cou'd do it, without altering the *Likeness*'. The hands, moreover, are always one of the most expressive elements in a work by Van Dyck.

Van Dyck's greatness as an artist, as well as a portrait painter, is most clearly seen in his double portraits and family groups, in which the elegance, fluency and tensions of the full-lengths are developed on a wider field. In the lustrous double portrait of the Stuart boys (no.44), or in his masterpiece on this scale, the double portrait of Lord Digby and Lord Russell (fig.30), the figures are twisted apart from each other. The tensions are eased by a masterly placing of rival attributes, and the billowing curtain and firm, stabilizing architecture emphasize the main thrusts of the composition. On a far larger scale these varying pulls within a composition, and

27

Fig.31 *The Family of Philip Herbert, 4th Earl of Pembroke.* The Earl of Pembroke

Fig.32 *Lady Mary Villiers with Charles Hamilton, Earl of Arran.* North Carolina Museum of Art

a rhythmical play of diagonals, link the members of the Pembroke family in the huge picture (fig.31) at Wilton: the first such picture to have been painted in such magnificent terms in this country. Immensely influential, it was never to be equalled by any of Van Dyck's successors. The actors are staged on a dais which is set parallel to the surface of the canvas; there are none of the full baroque recessions into a design which Rubens would have stressed on such a scale. In his approach to stagecraft, in, for instance, the architectural structure and the motif of the winged children on a cloud, the influence of Titian or Veronese is again predominant. The approach of the members of the family up to the apex of the design may have been developed from the main compositional lines of the *Vendramin Family*; and the isolated figure of Lady Mary Villiers, the daughter-in-law in white on the steps in the foreground, may be a reminiscence of the girl who stands half-way up the steps in Titian's *Christ before Pilate* in Vienna, which had been acquired by Lady Mary's father in 1621. Even in the portrait of Charles I in the hunting-field the King and the group composed of the horse and the equerry are raised on a low grassy stage.

In the *Pembroke Family* the flow of movement on the ground and in the sky, within a carefully constructed architectural framework, is as dramatic in a well-bred way as the courtly rhythms and sophisticated effects of a masque. The King is in the centre of the stage in Van Dyck's canvases, as he was in the more prosaic settings of Mytens or Pot, or in the masques designed in his honour by Inigo Jones and Ben Jonson to celebrate domestic and political felicity and the blessings of peace under his divinely guided rule; but the illusion is more subtle, and therefore infinitely more lasting in effect, in the hands of Van Dyck. He was never seemingly interested in complicated iconographical statements, although in some of his portraits, in Ben Jonson's words, 'the garments and the ensignes deliver the nature of the person'. The royal actor is as carefully presented in his different parts by Van Dyck as he was, for instance, by Honthorst, who actually painted the King and Queen, as if in a masque, in the roles of Apollo and Diana; but in Van Dyck's productions the methods and techniques are much more subtle and more effective because, thanks to his powers of imagination and technique, the illusion of reality is so totally convincing; and because his portraits of the King and Queen are great works of art on any terms.

Like Honthorst, but with more refinement, Van Dyck painted some portraits in a mythological vein which slightly resemble, in appearance, Inigo Jones's costume drawings: Lord d'Aubigny (no.61); Lady Southampton in triumph over Death and Fortune; Lady Digby as Prudence (no.9); Lady Portland and Lady d'Aubigny as nymphs; a young woman (no.42) dressed up as Tasso's Erminia; or Lady Mary Villiers as Venus (fig.32) with the little Lord Arran as Cupid in attendance: one of the pictures cited, with particular admiration, by Bellori.[30]

Some of the allusions made by Van Dyck in his portraits are obvious; others remain obscure; most of them are lightly stressed. The most frequently displayed attributes are a group of roses or a rose-bush in flower. The rose, as a symbol, can be interpreted in so many ways that it is impossible to explain the use of the symbol precisely in each instance. The rose on its branch, which stands behind Mrs Kirke (no.35) or is being plucked by Lady Wharton (no.52), for example, probably alludes to the association of a sweet smell with a sharp thorn, to the importance of achieving virtue through hardship. The rose when plucked and dried gives off its richest scent, so the love represented by this gesture may be, in the sitter's heart, of special intensity; and Hawkins in his *Parthenia Sacra* (1633) describes the rose as the 'chiefest grace of Spouses on their Nuptial dayes'. The scattered roses could refer to such broader concepts as beauty, innocence, virginity, marriage or premature death. Those held downwards above the womb by Lady Rich (no.33) and Lady Peterborough (no.34) probably refer to their hopes of issue.

In planning so large and complex a composition as the *Pembroke Family* Van Dyck might have produced a sketch in oil, as he did later for the *Garter Procession* (no.43). He made such sketches, however, with far less regularity than Rubens and relied chiefly on drawings in preparing a picture. Even so big and important a commission as the first equestrian portrait of the King was, it seems, first sketched on paper (no.68). According to the miniaturist Richard Gibson, who may have seen him at work and was in fact in the service of the Earl of Pembroke, Van Dyck, when a new sitter had arrived in the studio at Blackfriars, 'would take a little piece of blue paper upon a board before him, & look upon the Life & draw his figures & postures all in Suden lines, as angles with black Chalk & heighten with white chalke'.[31] A quantity of such sheets survive on which the first ideas for a new portrait are hurriedly set down or on which a section of a figure or a piece of drapery is studied independently. There is sometimes a lively impression of a sitter's appearance and personality in drawings made when he or she first sat or stood in the studio, when the design of the portrait was being discussed, or when Van Dyck was quietly thinking about a new commission.

Eberhard Jabach, who knew Van Dyck and was painted by him in London, recorded a conversation in which Van Dyck described his methods of work at this late point in his career. He had been forced to produce pictures far more rapidly than in his earlier days, when he had worked with infinite pains on his pictures in order to earn his bread and establish his reputation. The methods established in the studio at Blackfriars were adopted by Van Dyck's successors from Lely onwards. His clients in London sat to him, by appointment, for an hour at a time, whatever stage their portrait had reached. When the sitting was over, another would be arranged and, after a servant had cleaned the painter's brushes, the next sitter would be announced. Van Dyck could, by this method, work on several portraits on the same day. When he had lightly sketched out his first thoughts for a portrait, he would put the sitter in the chosen posture and within a quarter of an hour would have completed the drawing on the 'little piece of blue paper'. The design could then be laid out on the canvas by assistants. A drawing such as no.76 is squared so that they would not find it too difficult to transpose a particularly complicated piece in a design. The costume chosen by the sitter would be sent down to the studio so that it, too, so far as they were able, could be painted by the assistants. Then, in Jabach's words, Van Dyck *'repassoit legerement dessus, & y mettoit en très peu de tems, par son intelligence, l'art & la verité que nous y admirons'*.[32] Sir John Suckling provides a delightful vignette of Van Dyck in his studio: 'with all his fine colours and Pensills about him, his Frame, and right Light, and every thing in order'.[33] On many of his canvases one can see, from an aura of thicker paint or slightly discordant tone round the head, the section worked on when the client was actually sitting for the likeness.

William Sanderson, a slightly older contemporary of Van Dyck, who published his *Graphice* in 1658, claimed that Van Dyck had been the first painter 'that e're put Ladies dresse into a *careless Romance*'.[34] The women painted by Van Dyck seldom wear ordinary day dress; and Van Dyck, for the student of costume, is a less useful source than a more conventional painter such as Mytens or Johnson. He developed that sweet disorder in the dress which Lely was to paint so often. Many of Van Dyck's male sitters also affect a relaxed picturesque attire which was not too rigidly fashionable and helped to lift them, in mood, out of a too close association with the times in which they were painted. On occasion he would, for a special reason, paint a sitter (eg no.61) in an obviously Arcadian vein. Of course many of his male sitters wear contemporary dress, armour or, in one case, Garter robes, and it is noticeable that Van Dyck's royal sitters, especially the children, are almost invariably seen in contemporary costume. He paid, however, great attention to jewellery and he was a particularly accurate painter of such details as a sword-hilt.[35] It is clear from Lady Sussex's letters that she would like to have been painted wearing a fur set with diamonds which she had seen, probably, in another portrait. The jewels she eventually wore in the portrait were richer than those she owned, but she thought it no great matter if future ages thought her richer than she actually was. This suggests that some fairly grand accessories, notably the length of Italian velvet which was used to such effect in the background of a number of portraits, were kept by Van Dyck in the studio and could be offered to sitters as embellishments to a portrait.

The methods described by Jabach had been evolved so that Van Dyck could cope with the demands of a big and demanding practice. As his life drew to an end the physical and psychological pressures on him must have become almost unbearable, and they undoubtedly affected his work. At first sight his English pictures seem in general lighter in tone than the work of the Flemish or Italian periods, but the background of a portrait such as the young Prince Rupert (fig.17), painted before Van Dyck's arrival in London, is painted already in a high key and it is in fact the bright colours of the costumes worn by so many of his English sitters which cause the English portraits, to give, as a whole, so light an impression. Most of the sitters in his early portraits had been painted in dark colours. In England Van Dyck still used black to great effect, but developed in addition a lovely Veronese-like range of blues, greens, pinks, scarlets, silvers, golds and whites.

In quality there are certain tendencies discernible in the English period as a whole. If, for example, the equestrian portrait of the King in 1633 (no.11) is compared with the Prince of Orange's marriage portrait of 1641 (no.62), it can be seen that a style of refined perception, delicate touch, rich texture and subtle atmosphere has, under pressure, deteriorated. The methods are still very competent and the drawing impeccable; but the colour is pallid and the texture coarse or disturbingly thin. 'The *Colouring* is weak', to quote De Piles, 'and falls into the *Lead*; nevertheless his *Pencil* is happy every where'. It is remarkable that Van Dyck remained as consistent as he did; but as the English period drew to a close he must have relied more and more on his assistants. The draperies of, for example, *Lady Borlase* (no.50) are satisfactorily designed, but were perhaps not enlivened by Van Dyck. The canvas has, therefore, none of the shimmering beauty we see in, for instance, the portrait of the Countess of Bedford (no.41). In London Van Dyck would rarely have lavished on a head, except perhaps when painting a particularly important likeness of the King or Queen, such attention as he gave to his sitters in his earlier years;[36] but in, for example, his groups of the royal children (nos.18 and 26), quality and tonal harmonies are marvellously sustained throughout a complete design. There is an interesting variation in handling among the portraits of his English years. Almost to the end he could devote infinite pains to painting a special head – the three faces of the King, for example, in no.22, the grave head of *Pembroke* (no.12), the smiling face of Langlois (no.10); or the studies of the Queen for Bernini (nos.53 and 54). In certain portraits, such as the two ladies (no.29) in the National Gallery, the draperies are carefully and almost smoothly worked; but at the same time he could paint both heads and dresses with much greater freedom, and with a broken, nervous touch and superb Venetian bravura, in, for instance, *Hanmer* (no.37), the full-length *Strafford* (no.15), the *Earl of Denbigh* (no.16) or *Lord Arundel with his grandson* (no.21). And a composition, such as the two ladies, would be enriched with lovely passages of genre or still life, fresh in handling and exquisite in colour. To compare the landscape background in the portrait of the Wharton girls (no.56) with that behind Sir William Killigrew (no.38) is to be aware how tired the painter must have become; and in portraits like the *Duke of Hamilton* or *Lord d'Aubigny* (nos.60 and 61) the enlivening touches in figure, background and foreground are not sufficiently vivid, compared with the wonderfully spontaneous handling of the foliage in *Lord Denbigh* (no.16), to bring the composition completely to life. Consideration, however, would have been given as to where, and at what height, the portrait would originally have been hung.

Van Dyck must have been responsible also for organizing the production of copies of his portraits. The men who, in Lady Sussex's phrase, copied out Van Dycks, may not necessarily have been working under his roof; and the artists who were probably involved in such work, Jan van Belcamp, Remigius van Leemput and Geldorp, may have achieved a certain independence. Copies in miniature were also in production from 1632 onwards, and Van Dyck had to assess the competence of the miniaturists concerned. John Hoskins particularly was employed in this field from as early as 1632; but the most prized copies after Van Dyck on a small scale were made by Jean Petitot in enamel. It was said of a lesser miniaturist that his work fell as far short of

Fig.33 *Self-portrait with Endymion Porter*. Museo del Prado, Madrid

Petitot's as Johnson's had of Van Dyck's.[37]

Van Dyck's sitters came inevitably from a comparatively small world, but they came from court and country alike. Nearest to the royal family were those who were bound by ties of blood, affection, interest or religion to Van Dyck's royal patrons and were to devote themselves without hesitation to the King's cause in the Civil War. The Stuart brothers (nos.44, 48 and 61) or the courtiers, the Killigrews and Endymion Porter, for instance, are notable examples of this group. In 1633 the Queen had actually invited Van Dyck's brother, Canon Theodore van Dyck, to take up a post in her ecclesiastical household. Some of Van Dyck's most interesting and generous patrons, however, were to be found among men who mistrusted or disliked the King and Queen, disapproved strongly of the King's policies, especially of Laudianism and Charles's enfeebled foreign policy, and were to move into opposition to him. The Earl of Northumberland felt increasingly that the King had treated him badly; Pembroke unashamedly deserted him. Some of Van Dyck's finest portraits were done for such powerful and Puritan figures as the Earl of Warwick, the Earl of Bedford and his son, Lady Peterborough (no.34), Lord Danby (no.20) and Arthur Goodwin (no.55); and the patron who, despite Aubrey's claim for Lord Pembroke, probably owned the largest number of pictures by him was the Puritan Lord Wharton.

Van Dyck would perhaps have been most at ease in London with friendly, idiosyncratic and witty men like Sir Theodore de Mayerne, with whom he could talk

Fig.34 *The Family of Count John of Nassau-Siegen.* Viscount Gage

Fig.35 *Prince Thomas of Savoy.* Galleria Sabauda, Turin

about his methods and materials, Suckling, Endymion Porter and Kenelm Digby. In a unique and charming tribute of friendship he painted himself with Porter (Frontispiece and fig.33): a slight figure in black against the bulk of his bluff and ruddy-cheeked friend clothed in silver. Digby had been a friend for many years and may have been influential in persuading Van Dyck to return to London in 1632; he later gave Bellori information about the painter's London years. He commissioned a family group, a fairly misleading allegory (no.9) of his wife's virtues and a portrait of himself in mourning for her. He had actually summoned Van Dyck, 'the second day after she was dead', to paint his wife before she was 'folded up in her last sheete'.[38]

It is clear, however, that Van Dyck had never intended to settle permanently in London. In December 1633 his former patron, the Archduchess Isabella, had died. Philip IV appointed as her successor his brother the Cardinal-Infante Ferdinand. Van Dyck, perhaps anxious to recommend himself to a new patron on old ground, returned to Flanders in the spring of 1634. The new ruler did not, in fact, enter Brussels until November, after his victory over the Swedes, and artistic life in the province thereafter must have been dominated by the preparation of the triumphal arches which were to be erected in Antwerp for his official entry – the *Pompa Introitus Ferdinandi* – on 17 April 1635. Van Dyck played no part in this project; once again, perhaps, he found himself overshadowed by the overwhelming personality of Rubens. He had painted an official portrait of the Cardinal-Infante, but was unwilling to provide the artists, who were preparing the paintings for the arches and badly needed an approved likeness, with a copy of it at a reasonable price. The pictures he painted in these months in Flanders – Van Dyck was back in London by June 1635 – are, as a group, unsurpassed in scale and quality by those from any other period of his career. He painted a group (destroyed in 1695) for the Town Hall in Brussels; the group (fig.34) of the Nassau-Siegen family, the most baroque of all his large compositions of this kind, and a Berninesque equestrian portrait of Prince

33

Fig.36 *The Lamentation*. Alte Pinakothek, Munich

Thomas of Savoy (fig.35), Captain-General of the Spanish troops in the Netherlands. To these months also belongs his most refined late religious composition
(fig.36). The great full-length of the Abbé Scaglia (no.17) is an example of the
exceptionally high quality of his work as portrait painter in these crowded months.

   In October 1635, a few months after Van Dyck's return to London, the canvases
painted by Rubens for the Banqueting House arrived from Antwerp. Late in 1639
negotiations were initiated for a second series of canvases, this time for the Queen's
Bedchamber at Greenwich. The negotiations were carried out by Scaglia and
Gerbier and the artist chosen was Jordaens. Van Dyck had, however, painted at
least one piece for Greenwich which, at £100, is listed in his 'Memoire'. He had
received a grant of denization in March 1638, although he had purchased a
property in Flanders, but in September 1640 he secured a pass to travel. In
October he was in Antwerp once more. Rubens had died on 20 May and Van Dyck,
as the unquestioned head of the Flemish school, may have been impatient to return.
On his arrival he was asked by the Cardinal-Infante to finish for the King of Spain a
set of four pictures which had been commissioned from Rubens. Van Dyck, whom
the Cardinal-Infante described as so great a painter and a disciple of Rubens, would
only consent to paint an entirely independent picture to complete the series. Before
returning to London he had absolutely refused to touch the uncompleted canvases or
to work up the fourth on the basis of Rubens's sketch. The Cardinal-Infante
considered him to be entirely lacking in judgement.[39] In January 1641 he was in
Paris, where he hoped to secure the commission to decorate the *Grande Galerie* of the
Louvre; but in March Poussin received from Louis XIII a brief which gave him

34

control over the decoration of all the French King's palaces. Van Dyck was back in London in May to paint the Princess Royal and her husband (no.62), but he was by now very ill and found it increasingly difficult to meet demands for repetitions of his most recent royal portraits. It must have been a fearful time in which to attempt to work in London. The basis of royal authority and of the society in which Van Dyck had worked, and which he had so brilliantly recorded, the stability on which his practical and emotional welfare depended, were collapsing around him. The Long Parliament had assembled on 3 November 1640 and within ten months had brought about a constitutional and legal revolution. Strafford, one of Van Dyck's greatest patrons, was executed on 12 May 1641; an assault was launched on the King's chief advisers, among them Hamilton and Laud; there were outbreaks of violence by the London mob; at the end of the year the Irish Rebellion broke out and the Grand Remonstrance was passed. Smaller tragedies, such as the drowning of Mrs Kirke (no.35), must have seemed all too much like the nightmare horrors of discord in a masque, the dread of those who had sung of the charms of the halcyon years.[40] On 16 November Van Dyck was once more in Paris, seriously ill and asking for a passport to England for himself, his five servants and his coach.[41] 'Weake of body', he made his will on 4 December.[42] On 9 December he died, eight days after the birth of his daughter, the only child of his marriage (on 27 February 1640) to Mary Ruthven, a granddaughter of the 1st Earl of Gowrie. He was buried two days later in the choir of St Paul's Cathedral, near the tomb of John of Gaunt.

The oil sketch of the *Garter Procession* is all that survives of a scheme which might have satisfied Van Dyck's ambition to be regarded as a decorative, historical painter in the tradition of the school in which he had been brought up; he had hoped to be entrusted with another cycle of pictures in the Long Gallery of the Louvre. The sketch is evidence of a desire to escape from the arduous routine of the portrait practice; and the landscape drawings may also have provided a little relief. That the Garter scheme came to nothing makes the panel all the more poignant as a record of a scene in which the King and his Knights take part in the ancient ceremony which symbolizes a divinely ordered society. 'The glories of our blood and state are shadows not substantial things'; Van Dyck was painting for the King one last splendid illusion. It is also the last occasion when we see Van Dyck laying out his stage for his actors, as if in the last moments of a masque, in the full Venetian manner; and the sketch evokes once more the inevitable association which so many educated contemporaries had noticed. To a slightly later observer, a written description of the Garter ceremonies was 'like the designes & first Shadowings of some curiously intended Pourtraict which are not at the present Enriched with that beauty which the ultima manus or the accomplishing Art of the famous Titiano or van Dike did afterwards adde unto it'.[43] De Piles's assessment, in the English translation, could hardly be bettered: 'If his Performances are not alike perfect, all in the last degree, they carry with them, however, a *Great Character of Spirit, Nobleness, Grace* and *Truth*, insomuch that one may say of him, that excepting *Titian* only *Vandyck* surpasses all the *Painters* that went before him, or have come after him, in Portraits'.[44]

Notes to the Introduction

[1] The letter, which is in Italian, is among the Arundel Castle MSS (autograph letters, no.244). The late Duke of Norfolk kindly provided me with a photograph of it. It is printed in translation in Hervey, pp.175-6.

[2] *The Letters of Peter Paul Rubens*, ed. Ruth S. Magurn (Cambridge, Mass., 1955), pp.59-61.

[3] *Original unpublished Papers illustrative of the Life of Sir Peter Paul Rubens*, ed. W. N. Sainsbury (1859), p.54: a fuller text than in Hervey, p.186.

[4] See Sainsbury, op. cit. pp.54-8; Magurn, op. cit. pp.76, 446. Van Dyck's expertise was later to be useful to connoisseurs at the Stuart court, whose discernment he much respected (see R. W. Lightbown, 'Van Dyck and the Purchase of Paintings for the English Court', *Burl. Mag.*, vol.CXI (1969), pp.418-21.

[5] Other examples in this country of Van Dyck's early subject-pictures are: *The Betrayal of Christ* at Corsham Court and *St Martin dividing his Cloak* at Windsor.

[6] Hookham Carpenter, p.9.

[7] Ibid. p.10.

[8] Bellori, p.255.

[9] M. De Maeyer, *Albrecht en Isabella en de Schilderkunst* (Brussels, 1955), pp.193-4, 387. The probable original of the portrait is Glück, 299.

[10] See Millar, no.162.

[11] Hookham Carpenter, pp.24-6.

[12] J. G. van Gelder, 'Anthonie van Dyck in Holland in de zeventiende Eeuw', *Bulletin*, Musées Royaux des Beaux-Arts, Brussels, vol.VIII (1959), pp.43-86.

[13] Magnificent examples of Van Dyck's style at this date, but on a grander scale, are the portraits in the Wallace Collection of Philippe Le Roy (1630) and his wife (1631).

[14] Hookham Carpenter, p.71.

[15] Ibid. pp.28, 32, 70; Mary Edmond, 'Limners and Picturemakers', *Walpole Soc.*, vol. XLVII (1980), pp.125, 203, n.296.

[16] Vertue, vol.I, p.101.

[17] Hookham Carpenter, pp.29, 65.

[18] Ibid. pp.67-8, 71-4. These references should be treated with caution as it is not always clear when a specific payment was completed. A payment of £300 on 23 December 1637 was the remainder of £1200 due to the painter; £300 paid on 18 July 1637 was also part of this same debt (P.R.O., T.56/4, Warrants 1637-9, kindly communicated by Mr K. Timings).

[19] This portrait is imaginatively discussed in R. Strong, *Van Dyck: Charles I on Horseback* (1972).

[20] The most obvious instance of this is his transformation of a double portrait of the King and Queen by Mytens into his own double portrait of them which was painted for Somerset House and is now at Kremsier (see Millar, no.119).

[21] Bellori, pp.260, 264.

[22] Obituary notice by Baldwin Hamey (MS in the Royal College of Physicians) kindly communicated to me by Mr David Piper.

[23] Hookham Carpenter, p.71; *Van der Doort*, p.174; Wethey, vol.III (1975), p.235.

[24] The inventory is published by J. Müller-Rostock in *Zeitschrift für bildende Kunst*, vol.XXXIII (Leipzig, 1922), pp.22-4. See J. Ingamells, '"Perseus and Andromeda": the provenance', *Burl. Mag.*, vol.CXXIV (1982), pp.396-7 (I believe Northumberland would have resented the sobriquet, 'pragmatic roundhead'); and C. Gould's notes on the provenance of the National Gallery pictures in *The Sixteenth-Century Venetian School*, National Gallery (1959).

[25] R. W. Goulding and C. K. Adams, *Catalogue of the Pictures . . . at Welbeck Abbey . . .* (1936), p.485. The letter is dated February 1637.

[26] Thomas Randolph, 'On a Maid, seen by a Scholar in Somerset [House] Garden', *Poetical and Dramatick Works*, ed. W. C. Hazlitt (1875), p.661. Later in the poem: 'away she slipp'd, And in a fount her whitest hand she dipp'd', like a number of Van Dyck's ladies.

[27] British Library, Harl. MS 1636, f.102. When his collection of pictures was shipped over to the Low Countries in 1645, they included '7 groote conterfeytselen van van Dyck selven, alle tot de knien ende van de grootste vrouwen van Engelaand'. (*Na Peter Pauwel Rubens*, ed. J. Denucé (Antwerp, 1949), pp.34-5.)

[28] *Memoirs of the Verney Family during the Civil War*, compiled by Frances P. Verney (1892), vol.I, pp.257-61.

[29] *Memoirs of Princess Sophia, Electress of Hanover*, translated by H. Forester (1888), p.13.

[30] Bellori, p.262.

[31] British Library, Add. MS 22950, f.15. The passage is cited on p.320 of M. K. Talley, *Portrait Painting in England: Studies in the Technical Literature before 1700* (1981), in which much information on Van Dyck's technical methods is to be found.

[32] Jabach's information was given to De Piles and recorded in the latter's *Cours de Peinture par Principes* (Paris, 1708), pp.291-3. The account of Van Dyck's method in Bellori (pp.263-4) is substantially the same.

[33] *The Works of Sir John Suckling*, ed. T. Clayton (1971), p.121.

[34] *Graphice* (1658), p.19.

[35] Diana de Marly, 'Dress in Baroque Portraiture', *The Antiquaries Journal*, vol.LX, part II (1980), pp.268-84, is more concerned with the age of Lely, but is useful here; see also Sara Stevenson, 'Armour in Seventeenth-Century Portraits', *Scottish Weapons and Fortifications 1100-1800* (1981), pp.339-77. There is much information on the swords delineated by Van Dyck in A. V. B. Norman, *The Rapier and Small-Sword 1460-1820* (1980).

[36]Lanier is stated to have told Lely that Van Dyck had worked on his portrait, morning and afternoon, for seven days, that he had sat 'seven entire days for it', but was not allowed to see it until it was 'perfectly finished' (Vertue, vol.IV, p.169). This would account for the exceptional quality of the head in no. 6.

[37]*Memoirs of the Verney Family*, op. cit. (edn. of 1925), vol.I, p.472. See R. W. Lightbown, 'Jean Petitot and Jacques Bordier at the English Court', *The Connoisseur*, vol.168 (1968), pp.82–91; and J. Murdoch in *The English Miniature* (Yale University Press, 1981), p.101.

[38]Letter to his brother, 19 June 1633, printed in V. Gabrieli, *Sir Kenelm Digby* (Rome, 1957), pp.246–9. A good version of the picture is in the Dulwich Picture Gallery.

[39]*Correspondance de Rubens*, ed. M. Rooses and Ch. Ruelens, vol. VI (Antwerp, 1909), pp.310–12.

[40]This grim period is well summarized in ch.VII of P. Zagorin, *The Court and the Country* (1969).

[41]Van Dyck's original letter is now in the Fondation Custodia (Coll. F. Lugt), Institut Néerlandais, Paris. I am grateful to Carlos van Hasselt for providing me with a photograph of it.

[42]Hookham Carpenter, pp.75–7. His executors claimed that £850 was due to them from the Crown. After the Restoration his daughter Justina was granted an annual pension of £200.

[43]Fabian Philipps to Elias Ashmole, 27 January 1673 (*Elias Ashmole*, ed. C. H. Josten (1966), vol.IV, p.1302).

[44]De Piles, *The Art of Painting*, English translation (1706), p.306.

Bibliographical note

There is no up-to-date detailed survey of Van Dyck's English period. The only full-length life of the artist in English is Sir L. Cust, *Anthony van Dyck an Historical Study of his Life and Works* (1900), which remains useful. The most important and reliably illustrated study of the painter's life and work is the volume by G. Glück in the *Klassiker der Kunst* series (1931), but the section on the English period is now very much out of date. Glück, for example, did not include the pictures at Petworth, but these are covered in C. H. Collins Baker's *Catalogue* (1920) of the collection there. References to recent specialized literature will be found in the individual entries in this catalogue.

Glück provides (pp.516–17) a good bibliography for the earlier literature on Van Dyck. The most important early account of the English period is the life of Van Dyck in Bellori's *Vite* of 1672 (pp.253–64); short early accounts in English of his career are to be found in the English edition (1695) of Du Fresnoy's *De Arte Graphica* (pp.330–2) and in B. Buckeridge's *Essay towards an English School of Painters*, added to the English translation (1706) of De Piles, *The Art of Painting* (pp.303–6, 469–72). For the English period there is a mass of material in the *Notebooks* of George Vertue (see the Abbreviations), from which Horace Walpole partly constructed his account of the artist's career (*Anecdotes of Painting*, ed. J. Dallaway and R. N. Wornum (1888), vol. I, pp.316–38); in part III (1831) and the Supplement, part IX (1842), of J. Smith, *A Catalogue Raisonné of the Works of the most eminent Dutch, Flemish and French Painters*; and in G. F. Waagen, *Treasures of Art in Great Britain*, 3 vols. (1854). The material on Van Dyck in the two manuscript volumes in the Louvre, compiled at the end of the eighteenth century, is conveniently presented by E. Larsen, *La Vie, les ouvrages et les élèves de Van Dyck* (Brussels, 1974).

W. Hookham Carpenter published in his *Pictorial Notices . . .* (1844) a number of the most important contemporary documents relating to Van Dyck. Those that have since come to light are cited in this catalogue.

The most recent attempt to produce a fully-illustrated catalogue of the artist's paintings is the *Catalogo delle Opere* in two volumes by E. Larsen (Milan, 1980) in the *Classici dell'Arte* series. This is not wholly reliable. L. van Puyvelde's work on the English period is summarized in his *Van Dyck* (Brussels and Amsterdam, 1950). The artist's drawings, on the other hand, have been very well covered in H. Vey, *Die Zeichnungen Anton van Dycks* (Brussels, 1962); and the same author published a useful survey of the oil sketches in the *Bulletin* of the Musées Royaux des Beaux-Arts in Brussels (2–3 (1956), pp.167–208). There is much information on the painter's technical methods in M. K. Talley, *Portrait Painting in England: Studies in the Technical Literature before 1700* (1981).

Any student who has undertaken to work on an artist and his *œuvre* will know that it is only through the detailed examination involved in making a *catalogue raisonné* that he will acquire a full awareness at least of the main problems; and much detailed information on Van Dyck will be found in the catalogues of the Flemish School in the National Gallery by G. Martin (1970), of the Van Dycks in The Hermitage by M. Varshavskaya (1963) and of the Tudor, Stuart and Early Georgian Pictures in the Royal Collection by O. Millar (1963). Much detailed information will be found in the catalogues of exhibitions of Van Dyck's work in the Nottingham University Art Gallery (1960), at Agnew's (1968) and in The Queen's Gallery (1968); and in the catalogue of the exhibition of *Flemish Art* at the Royal Academy, 1953–4. A good selection of plates of the work of Van Dyck and his older and younger contemporaries in England is to be found in the catalogue, *The Age of Charles I*, Tate Gallery (1972).

Although the themes are not directly connected with the painter's English years, the student should consult two excellent catalogues: J. R. Martin and G. Feigenbaum, *Van Dyck as Religious Artist*, Art Museum, Princeton University (1979), and A. McNairn, *The Young Van Dyck*, National Gallery of Canada (1980). Van Dyck's *Iconography* is exhaustively examined in M. Mauquoy-Hendrickx, *L'Iconographie d'Antoine Van Dyck* (Brussels, 1956).

For Van Dyck's place in the history of English painting the student should read Sir E. K. Waterhouse, *Painting in Britain 1530–1790* (1953; 3rd edn. 1969), and M. Whinney and O. Millar, *English Art 1625–1714* (1957). A sound account of Van Dyck's work in the Flemish context, but with a good assessment of the English period, is H. Gerson and E. H. Ter Kuile, *Art and Architecture in Belgium 1600–1800* (1960), pp.109–26.

A charming account of Van Dyck and his influence in England is D. Piper's lecture, 'Van Dyck in England', *Museums Journal*, vol.62, no.2 (1962), pp.85–99; see also the same author's short *Van Dyck* in the Fontana Unesco series (1968). The importance of Van Dyck's example for, in particular, Gainsborough, in the following century in England is well analysed by D. Cherry and J. Harris in 'Eighteenth-century portraiture and the seventeenth-century past', *Art History*, vol.5, no.3 (1982), pp.287–309. A very good account of the artist at court is in M. Levey, *Painting at Court* (1971), ch.4; Sir Michael's pages on Van Dyck's work for the King and Queen could not be bettered. Sir Roy Strong, in his *Van Dyck: Charles I on Horseback* (1972), produced a study, no less stimulating for being in part controversial, of one great royal portrait. A useful introduction to the art and atmosphere of the early Stuart court is G. Parry, *The Golden Age restor'd* (1981), in which there is (pp.219–25) an outstandingly good section on Van Dyck.

Catalogue notes

The paintings cannot all be catalogued in accurate chronological order. Those which are not securely dated have been placed in a suggested sequence, grouped with the dated portraits with which they can stylistically, perhaps, be associated.

It has not been possible to take fresh measurements of all the paintings and drawings and many of those given in the catalogue have been provided by owners and custodians. Measurements are given in centimetres and (in brackets) inches, height before width. For the catalogue of an exhibition held in the National Portrait Gallery it has seemed more important to provide biographical information on the sitters than to compile a detailed provenance for each picture. Wherever possible the origin of a picture has been described, but its later history is only briefly mentioned. Nor is there space in such a catalogue for a full list of copies or for long bibliographical references for each entry. The most recent important literary references have been cited and from these the student could compile a fuller bibliography.

The following abbreviations have been used:

Age of Charles I	O. Millar, *The Age of Charles I Painting in England 1620–1649*, Tate Gallery (1972)
Agnew, 1968	*Van Dyck A loan exhibition of pictures and sketches principally from private collections*, Thomas Agnew and Sons Ltd (1968)
Aubrey	*Aubrey's Brief Lives*, ed. O. Lawson Dick (edn. of 1962)
Bellori	G. P. Bellori, *Le Vite de' Pittori, Scultori et Architetti Moderni* (Rome. 1672)
Burl. Mag.	*The Burlington Magazine*
Clarendon	Earl of Clarendon, *The History of the Rebellion and Civil Wars in England*, ed. W. D. Macray, 6 vols. (1888)
Collins Baker, *Petworth*	C. H. Collins Baker, *Catalogue of the Petworth Collection of Pictures* (1920)
Corbett and Norton	M. Corbett and M. Norton, *Engraving in England in the Sixteenth & Seventeenth Centuries*, part III (1964)
Glück	G. Glück, *Van Dyck Des Meisters Gemälde, Klassiker der Kunst* (Stuttgart, 1931)
Hervey	Mary F. S. Hervey, *The Life Correspondence & Collections of Thomas Howard Earl of Arundel* (1921)
Hookham Carpenter	W. Hookham Carpenter, *Pictorial Notices: consisting of a Memoir of Sir Anthony Van Dyck* (1844)
Larsen	E. Larsen, *L'opera completa di Van Dyck, Classici dell'Arte*, 2 vols. (Milan, 1980)
Martin, *Catalogue*	G. Martin, *The Flemish School c.1600–c.1900*, National Gallery (1970)
Millar	O. Millar, *The Tudor, Stuart and early Georgian Pictures in the Collection of Her Majesty The Queen* (1963)
N.P.G.	National Portrait Gallery
P.	G. Parthey, *Wenzel Hollar Beschreibendes Verzeichniss seiner Kupferstiche* (Berlin, 1853)
Piper, 1963	D. Piper, *Catalogue of Seventeenth-Century Portraits in the National Portrait Gallery 1625–1714* (1963)
P.R.O.	Public Record Office
R.A., 1953–4	*Flemish Art 1300–1700*, Royal Academy (1953–4)
Sale	'The Inventories and Valuations of the King's Goods 1649–1651', ed. O. Millar, *Walpole Society*, vol.XLIII (1972)
Van der Doort	'Abraham van der Doort's Catalogue of the Collections of Charles I', ed. O. Millar, *Walpole Society*, vol.XXXVII (1960)
Varshavskaya	M. Varshavskaya, *Van Dyck Paintings in The Hermitage* (Leningrad, 1963); text in Russian
Vertue	G. Vertue, *Notebooks*, 5 vols., *Walpole Society*, vol.XVIII (1930), vol.XX (1932), vol.XXII (1934), vol.XXIV (1936), vol.XXVI (1938); and index, vol.XXIX (1947)
Vey	H. Vey, *Die Zeichnungen Anton van Dycks*, 2 vols. (Brussels, 1962)
Vey, *Ölskizzen*	H. Vey, 'Anton van Dycks Ölskizzen', Musées Royaux des Beaux-Arts, Brussels, *Bulletin*, 2–3 (1956), pp.167–208
Warwick	Sir P. Warwick, *Memoires of the reigne of King Charles I* (1701)
Wethey	H. E. Wethey, *The Paintings of Titian*, 3 vols. (1969–75)

Paintings

1 Portrait of a Man, thought to be George Gage (c.1592–1638), with two Attendants

1620.

Canvas, 115×113.5 (45¼×44¹¹⁄₁₆)

Three-quarter-length, leaning on an altar-like structure on which two men hold up, apparently for inspection, an antique (?) statue of a woman (?).

The authorship of the group and the identity of the principal sitter have given rise to controversy for many years. Formerly in the collection of Sir Joshua Reynolds, the picture was described as a portrait of Rubens with two other artists, and considered to be by Van Dyck, when it was sold in Reynolds's sale at Christie's, 17 March 1795 (73); it was bought by Angerstein, in whose collection it was bought for the National Gallery in 1824.

The side of the structure on which the statue is being placed is decorated with a coat of arms of which only the upper part is visible, but which displays the first and second quarters of the arms borne by the Gage family: the saltire and the sun in splendour. The prominent and luxuriantly carved ram's head could be an allusion to the same family, whose crest is a ram's head. The sitter may therefore be George Gage, a younger son of Edward Gage of Firle, a diplomat and 'a graceful person, of good address, well skill'd in musick, painting, and architecture; a master of several languages'. He bought pictures for the Duke of Buckingham and as early as 1616 was negotiating with Rubens, on behalf of Sir Dudley Carleton, for pictures. He was also in touch, in the following year, with other Antwerp painters. He was planning to visit Rubens in Antwerp once more early in 1620. He must have met the young Van Dyck – perhaps on a number of occasions – and it could be argued that no.1 was painted in 1620, not long before Van Dyck paid his first visit to London; and if Gage was in London in the winter of 1620–1, it could have been painted in England.

Gregory Martin was reluctant to accept the identification and authorship of the group (*Catalogue*, pp.58–61), but the bold, rather superficial, handling, the loose construction of many of the elements in the design and of the group itself, the careless or misunderstood anatomy, are all entirely characteristic of Van Dyck's style *c.*1620–1; when he had broken down the rigid pattern in which his earlier portraits had been set (they had also been painted almost invariably on panel) and had begun to introduce architectural backgrounds and a glimpse of a landscape. These elements are displayed in a more restrained vein in the portrait of *Arundel* (no.2). The gesture of the sitter's right arm is reminiscent of the gesture made by the father in the *Family Group* of the same date (Glück, 112); and the boneless, hanging left hand is equally typical of Van Dyck at this date. If the sitter is really George Gage, the composition may be intended to refer to his dealings on behalf of the collectors at Whitehall; and its informal, 'conversation' air is a remarkable innovation in the development of the baroque portrait (O. Millar, 'Notes on three Pictures by Van Dyck', *Burl. Mag.*, vol.cxi (1969), pp.414–17).

The Trustees of the National Gallery

2 (detail)

After Van Dyck's return to London in 1632, the Earl of Arundel became again one of his most important patrons (see the excellent treatment and bibliography in A. McNairn, *The Young van Dyck*, National Gallery of Canada (1980), no.65).

Rebecca Pollard Logan, USA

2

2 Thomas Howard, 2nd Earl of Arundel (1585–1646)

Canvas, 113×80 (44×31½)

Three-quarter-length, seated, holding in his right hand a paper and in his left hand the Lesser George, the badge of the Garter suspended from the ribbon of the Order.

The Earl, an almost legendary figure in the history of connoisseurship in England, had been one of the first to be informed (see above, p.10), from Antwerp, in the summer of 1620, of Van Dyck's success; and he was involved, early in 1621, in the formalities of arranging Van Dyck's journey to Italy. It is natural, therefore, to assume that no.2 was painted during the artist's first visit to the English court. In style it can confidently be placed in those months. It has the sense of space, ease and latent movement which were displayed in the portrait of George Gage(?) (no.1). It is perhaps the first of the relaxed, seated, basically neo-Venetian, portraits which were to become a standard element in Van Dyck's repertory (no.12 is a good late instance of the same convention), with a new liveliness in, for example, the handling of the landscape and the movement of the curtain which is probably the first in the painter's *œuvre* to have a woven pattern.

There is no contemporary evidence for the tradition that the portrait was presented by the sitter to the Duke of Buckingham. It was eventually in the Orléans collection and was subsequently purchased by the Duke of Bridgewater; later in the Gans (Frankfurt), Baschstitz, Guggenheim (New York) and Lenyon collections.

3 The Continence of Scipio

Canvas, 183×232.5 (72×91½)

The story, as told by Livy (bk.XXVI.50), is a famous tribute to the virtues of generosity and continence and was held up by Macchiavelli as a model of astute statecraft. Scipio Africanus, after he had captured Carthago Nova in 209 B.C., released a beautiful female captive, restored her to Allucius, to whom she was betrothed, and gave to the fortunate pair the gifts her parents had brought as ransom.

No.3 is thought to be the picture recorded in the Duchess of Buckingham's inventory (1635) as hanging in the hall of York House: 'Vandyke One great Peice being Scipio'; and, at an unspecified date, the Duke of Buckingham had made, through Endymion Porter, payment to Van Dyck. Stylistically the picture can confidently be placed in the period when Van Dyck, in the winter of 1620–1, was working for a few months at the English court. The fragment of a frieze, lying rather awkwardly in the lower left corner, has been identified by John Harris as a Roman provincial relief, recently discovered on the site of Arundel House. It may have been acquired by Arundel after the Duke's assassination in 1628. It has been suggested that the subject contains an allusion to the marriage of Buckingham which had taken place on 16 May 1620.

The composition, and many of the elements in the design, are influenced by Rubens's treatment of the subject (c.1615–17), destroyed by fire in 1836 but recorded in engravings (see Agnes Czobor, 'An Oil Sketch by Cornelis de Vos', *Burl. Mag.*, vol.CIX (1967), pp.351–5; for Rubens's preliminary sketch, and a useful discussion, see J. Held, *The Oil Sketches of Peter Paul Rubens* (Princeton, 1980), vol.I, pp.385–6, no.287). Van Dyck's debt to Rubens is no less obvious in his preparatory drawings for the subject; and his (probably) final drawing (formerly in Bremen; Vey, no.107 recto) is as personal a reinterpretation of Rubens as the painting. The contrast between the temperaments, artistically and emotionally, of the two painters is particularly apparent in a comparison between the almost naked man with the vase, lower right, and the probable prototype in Rubens's magnificently sculptural nude figure in Rubens's *Abraham and Melchizedek* at Caen. The strange mood, the odd, undulating movements, the rather uneasy elegance, the lack of substance felt in construction and modelling alike and the superficial brilliance of much of the handling are stylistically what could be expected from the artist at this date, when he was moving so fast from the orbit of Rubens. There is already a marked contrast with such slightly earlier works as *Samson and Delilah* (fig.6) at Dulwich, and there are already indications of the qualities which were to develop fast in Italy.

3

The same mood – the same rather theatrical, ironical air –
can be sensed in *S. Ambrosius and the Emperor Theodosius* in
the National Gallery. The finished composition is also
influenced, especially in the way in which the action is
cramped into the foreground on to a narrow stage, by
Veronese: by, for example, his *Esther and Ahasuerus* (fig.5)
which was in Buckingham's collection (for a very good
discussion and full bibliography, see J. Byam Shaw, *Paintings by Old Masters at Christ Church Oxford* (1967) pp.125–6,
no.245; A. McNairn, *The Young van Dyck*, National Gallery
of Canada (1980), no.64).

The Governing Body, Christ Church, Oxford

4 Sir Robert Shirley (1581(?)–1628)

Canvas, 200×133.4 (79×52½)

c·1622

Inscribed: *S.ͬ Robert Shirley*

Full-length, standing, in Persian costume, holding a bow
and a quiver of arrows in his left hand. His tunic is of
silver, flecked with gold and with deep blue collar and pale
crimson bows. His cloak is pale gold, with blue ribbons,

richly embroidered with figures and flowers in a variety of
colours.

The sitter was an Englishman in the diplomatic service of
the Shah of Persia. Between 22 July and 29 August 1622
he was in Rome – with his wife (see no.5) – as Persian
Ambassador to Pope Gregory XV. Their presence in
Rome coincided with Van Dyck's first visit there and he
drew them both on separate pages of his Sketchbook (now
in the British Museum; ed. G. Adriani (Vienna, 1940),
pp.55–63, ff.60v–63). The drawing of Sir Robert is annotated with colour-notes: *'drapo doro/le figure et gli foliagi/de
colori differenti/de veluto'*.

The portraits mark something of a turning point in the
development of Van Dyck's style. The surfaces are richly
laden with paint, with much of the dragged, fluent quality
of, for example, the *Continence of Scipio*; but the flesh is
thinner and drier and the underpainting is now a deep
red-brown on Italian canvas of a coarse weave. The rapid
drawing of details, such as the top of the quiver, over this
deep tone, is identical with passages in more formal portraits of the Italian period, such as the *Young Man in Armour*
in Vienna (Glück, 178). The immensely exotic costumes,

44

4

and a reddish-brown robe covered with embroidery. Her head-dress is crowned with grey-black plumes. Beside her, on a blue cloth lined with gold, are a monkey and a book(?).

See no.4. Lady Shirley was a Circassian, daughter of Ishmael Khan. She was a Christian and had married Sir Robert before 1627. She retired to Rome after his death.

In Van Dyck's preliminary drawing in the Sketchbook Lady Shirley sits in much the same posture as in the finished portrait, but the landscape with a distant tower is placed to the left of her. Weaknesses in drawing and placing the hands still link the portrait with a number of those in the first Flemish period. The handling of such passages as the curtain, with its impasted silvery lights, is reminiscent of Tintoretto. A vivid patch of colour is provided by the table behind the sitter. The handling throughout is brilliant and direct, with a great variety of surface. The rich, sparklingly romantic, vein – the painter's fascination with the sitter's personality and exotic appearance – the glance of the sitter that rivets the attention, enhancing and transcending the splendour of her apparel: these are qualities that are to be developed in the great female full-lengths of the Genoese period (Agnew, 1968, no.18).

HM Treasury and the National Trust, Egremont Collection, Petworth

6 Nicholas Lanier (1588–1666)

Canvas, 111×87.5 (43$\frac{11}{16}$×34$\frac{7}{16}$)

Three-quarter-length, standing to the left, in a black cloak and a white doublet lined with pinkish scarlet; behind is a rusticated wall and a glimpse of landscape.

Member of a musical family of French origin – his grandfather had been a musician at the court of Henry II before coming to England – a fine singer and a leading figure in the musical life of his time: Musician-in-Ordinary for Lutes and Voices, Musician to the Prince of Wales (the future Charles I) and ultimately Master of the King's Music. He was involved as a designer, composer and performer in masques at court. The music for Ben Jonson's *Lovers Made Men* (1617), for example, 'was sung, after the Italian manner, *stilo recitativo*, by Master Nicholas Lanier, who ordered and made both the scene and the music', and was important in the evolution of opera. He was also active in artistic circles at court (Richard Symonds reported later that he had been '*inamorato di Artemisia Gentileschi, che pingeva bene*'). He was a very early lover, and collector, of drawings (in 1637 he was in correspondence with Langlois), and was employed by the King in the purchase of works of art. In particular, he played a prominent part in the acquisition of the Mantuan collection. He supervised the packing and dispatch of the collection by sea and himself escorted the most vulnerable pictures overland to Flanders. In June 1628 he arrived in Antwerp. Rubens wrote on 15 June that: 'The English gentleman who is taking the art collection of Mantua to England has arrived here'. It was presumably at this period that Van Dyck painted Lanier, with whose brother-in-law, Edward Norgate, he was first to lodge

brilliantly painted, create a magnificent glowing spectacle. The two portraits are only the second surviving pair of full-lengths in Van Dyck's career – they are the first to survive from the Italian period – and although in certain weaknesses of construction and in some aspects of their technical virtuosity they are reminiscent of his earlier Flemish style, they begin to reveal something of the grandeur of Van Dyck's Genoese full-lengths. The exotic costume is, incidentally, recorded in an unattributed full-length of the sitter at Berkeley Castle, which may have been painted slightly later in London.

The two portraits are described by Bellori (p.255: '*Antonio ritrasse questo Signore, e la moglie nell' habito persiano, accrescendo con la vaghezza de gli habiti peregrini la bellezza de' ritratti*'); they were in the collection of Lord Egremont at Petworth by 1815 (Agnew, 1968, no.17).

HM Treasury and the National Trust, Egremont Collection, Petworth

5 Teresia, Lady Shirley (1593–1668)

(COLOUR PLATE I, between pages 16 and 17)

Canvas, 200×133.4 (79×52$\frac{1}{2}$)

Full-length, seated, in Persian dress: a deep golden veil

6

7 Charles I and Queen Henrietta Maria with their two eldest Children, Charles, Prince of Wales, and Mary, Princess Royal

Canvas, 302.9×255.9 (119¼×100¾);[1] including additions made in painting of c.31.7 (12½) at the top and 21.6 (8½) on the right.

The King is seated on the left in black with the ribbon and star of the Garter. His doublet is richly laced with silver and his cloak is lined with pink. He holds a paper in his right hand which rests on a crimson table-cloth beside the Imperial Crown of State,[2] the orb and the sceptre. At his knee stands the little Prince of Wales, who had been born on 29 May 1630, in green 'coats' and apparently pointing to his little sister. On the right the Queen, in deep gold with blue bows, is seated beside the King, supporting in her arms the infant Princess (born on 4 November 1631) who wears a long white frock with a little gold chain. Between the King and Queen are two greyhounds; the small black and white hound is of the Italian breed of which the King's mother had been so fond. The royal pair are seated in two X-frame chairs of state.[3] Beyond the architectural background, across which is suspended a gold curtain and tassel, is a view of the Thames at Westminster with the Parliament House, Westminster Hall and (?) the Clock Tower.

A warrant was issued on 8 August 1632 for payments to Van Dyck which included £100 for 'One great peece of o[r] royall selfe, Consort and children'. It was placed by the King in the Long Gallery 'towards the Orchard' at Whitehall in a 'Carved Some part Guilded frame' (*Van der Doort*, p.42, giving measurements as 294.6×243.8 (116×96)).

At a later date the canvas was enlarged so that it could hang as a pendant to the equestrian portrait of the King (no.11). This may have been done when William III hung the two pictures in the Gallery at Kensington; but it is more likely to have happened in the reign of George III in whose time the pictures hung together in the Japan Room at Buckingham House. The frames for the two canvases are certainly of that date. In 1976 cleaning and restoration of the picture was initiated and in the course of the operation the canvas was reduced to its original size. The later additions to the canvas remain attached to it, but have been turned over.

As early as 1676 it was described as 'now allmost all pilled off' because it had been primed with pipe clay. Analysis carried out at the Hamilton Kerr Institute revealed that the ground does contain elements 'typical of Cornish china clay or of any other white clay formed by the natural weathering of plagioclase containing granite' (from report, dated 24 January 1979, by Mrs Pamela England). The canvas has a herring-bone weave with a pattern of coloured stripes and is much coarser than the artist's usual canvas which has the texture of fine linen. The painting will have been lined and cleaned on a number of occasions and these operations, combined with its original fragility, have brought about a substantial cumulative loss throughout the composition; but the recently completed cleaning and restoration, the reconstruction of the original proportions of the canvas and the

when he arrived in London four years later. It is impossible stylistically to place the portrait after 1632. For the preparatory drawing, see no.67.

There is a curiously nondescript passage in the lower left corner of the composition. The head, both in drawing and painting, is set rather oddly on the shoulders – it appears to float above them. The costume is very finely painted; and the head is treated with exceptional refinement and sensitivity, particularly round the eyes. The end of the brush is used in modelling the moustache.

The portrait entered the collection of Charles I and hung in the Bear Gallery at Whitehall next to a portrait, of the same scale and period, of the Antwerp organist Henri Liberti (*Van der Doort*, p.7). These two portraits of musicians would have shown the King how Van Dyck's style as a portrait painter was developing between the two English visits. At the sale of the King's goods Lanier himself bought the portrait (on the back of which, during recent restoration, the CR brand was revealed) for £10.

According to Bellori (p.262), Van Dyck also painted Lanier in the likeness of David harping before Saul. It is conceivable that a picture in the Musée de l'Hotel Sandelin, Saint-Omer (Inv.5921) may record part at least of this lost picture (*La Peinture Flamande au Temps de Rubens*, Lille, Calais, Arras (1977), no.33). (Much valuable information on Lanier is to be found in F. Lanier Graham, 'The Earlier Life and Work of Nicholas Lanier', unpublished thesis submitted to the Faculty of Philosophy, Columbia University, 1955.)

Kunsthistorisches Museum, Vienna

7

is, however, exceedingly perceptive and the rigidity of the design as a whole is relaxed by many passages of subtle movement and by the *rapport* established between the two principal sitters by the Queen's glance. The 'Great Piece' was probably the largest free-standing royal portrait group that had, at that time, been painted in England. Van Dyck's consummate skill lay in his ability to give an informal or domestic air to an immensely grand statement about the King and the early Stuart dynasty. It would have been natural to Van Dyck to design a strictly frontal composition if the group was to close a vista at the end of a long gallery and convey the illusion of a view through the wall behind the figures to an actual London scene.

Copies were soon in production. Remigius van Leemput was paid £50 for a copy in 1643 and a copy was at Hampton Court in 1649. When the original was back in its old position after the Restoration, Pepys (on 26 April 1667) saw a young man making a copy in pen and ink. A small early copy at Woburn may be by Leemput, who may also have painted the life-size copy now in the City Museum and Art Gallery in Birmingham. Other early copies are, for example, at Goodwood, at Raby, in the Devonshire collection and in the Royal Hospital, and there are many copies and derivations of individual parts of the design, although some of the copies of the single figures may have been made by cutting up copies of the whole.

The influence of the composition was immediate. Cornelius Johnson's group of the Capel family, painted in the late 1630s (N.P.G., no.4759), combines elements from the 'Great Piece' with the main iconographical theme of Honthorst's slightly earlier Buckingham family group; and it has been suggested that Rigaud's double portrait of M. Le Bret and his son was inspired by the copy of the 'Great Piece' which was then in the Orléans Collection (Ursula Hoff, *European Paintings before Eighteen Hundred*, National Gallery of Victoria (1967), pp.108–9), (R.A., 1953–4, no.160; Millar, no.150).

Her Majesty The Queen

[1] This is the measurement of the stretcher. The actual painted surface measures 298.1×250.8 (117⅜×98¾).

[2] In the collection of S.K.H. Prince Ernst August is a painting of the regalia exactly as it appears here. On a contemporary *cartellino* is an inscription: . . .*Corona Regis Anglia CAROLI. I Regina infelicissimilab Anthon. Van Dyck Equite, ad Vivum depicta;* but the handling is very restrained and the composition may have been copied from no.7 or from the double portrait of the King and Queen in Kremsier in Czechoslovakia in which the regalia appears in exactly the same arrangement.

[3] A chair from Hampton Court (but now at Knole) is very close to those painted by Van Dyck, even down to the arrangement of the studs on the boss which is placed over the crossing of the legs (P. Thornton, *Seventeenth-Century Interior Decoration in England, France and Holland* (1978), p.195, pl.168).

recreation of the scale of the figures established by Van Dyck in relation to the design as a whole, have restored much of the original appearance of the picture. Formerly it was only possible to assess the picture by studying the more reputable early copies.

Placed at the end of the Long Gallery at Whitehall it would have made, perhaps, as strong an impact on the visitor as the slightly later equestrian portrait (no.11) was to make at St James's. As a presentation of the early Stuart dynasty, a perceptive visitor might have recognized it as a sequel to Holbein's wall-painting of Henry VIII or to a piece from the school of Holbein (Millar, no.43), which is at Hampton Court and in which the royal family is grouped in rather the same way (although more formally and on a less impressive scale) and in which there is a view of Westminster through archways in the background. In Van Dyck's day this early picture was hanging in the Privy Gallery at Whitehall.

If payment was made to him on 8 August, Van Dyck must have started work on the 'Great Piece' soon after he arrived in London. A pencil sketch of the King (Vey, no.205) is probably a copy of his original thoughts for the position of the King and could record his first sitting from his new patron. The 'Great Piece' was, moreover, the first full-length family group Van Dyck had painted since he had left Italy and it is the most formal of all his large groups, with the massive architectural features behind the sitters and the authoritative placing of the King's hand on the table beside his regalia. The remote grandeur of the King is heightened by his costume. The paned doublet and the falling ruff are the same as those in which he had been painted a few years earlier by Mytens. The portrait

8

8 Queen Henrietta Maria (1609–69)

Canvas, 107.3×84.5 (42½×33½)

Three-quarter-length, in white, standing beside a table and resting her hand on a bunch of roses. Her crown is on a ledge beside her.

The payments made by the King to Van Dyck on 8 August 1632 included £20 for a portrait of 'our royall Consort'. This is thought to be the portrait in the royal collection (Millar, no.147) and recent cleaning has confirmed that it is a work of exceptional distinction (The Queen's Gallery, *Kings & Queens* (1982–4), no.31). It proved understandably to be a very popular image of the young Queen, who had probably in the King's eyes never been satisfactorily painted by Mytens; and there are a number of versions and variants of considerable quality which almost certainly would have been issued from Van Dyck's studio with his *imprimatur*. These include no.8 and versions in the possession of the Duke of Northumberland and Lord Cowdray. The pattern was used by Van Dyck, also in 1632, in composing the double portrait, now in Kremsier, of the King and Queen for Somerset House; from the head in that composition John Hoskins painted in 1632 the large miniature now in the Rijksmuseum; and that 'type' was superimposed on the earlier double portrait by Mytens (Millar, no.119) which had been almost unrecognizably recast by Van Dyck. There are innumerable inferior derivations from this pattern.

The principal difference between no.8 and the royal picture lies in the placing of the crown, which in the prototype stands on the table, and in the folds of the Queen's sleeve. The head and hands are probably rather worn, but the background is a fine example of a characteristically Van Dyckian harmony: blue and white in the sky against warm gold in the curtain.

The portrait was formerly at Blenheim and was in the Blenheim Palace sale at Christie's, 31 July 1886 (235); it was eventually acquired by Lord Wantage. In 1708 'un *portrait d'une reine d'Angleterre,* de Van Dyck' had been in a group of pictures which were given to the Duke of Marlborough in Brussels and had been formerly in the palace at Tervuren. This was a three-quarter-length which, with a companion portrait of Charles I, can be traced back to an inventory of 1659 (M. De Maeyer, *Albrecht en Isabella en de Schilderkunst* (Brussels, 1955), pp.436, 458, 461, 462).

Christopher Loyd, Esq

9 Venetia Stanley, Lady Digby (1600–33), as Prudence

Canvas, 99.7×79.4 (39¼×31¼)

Seated, full-length, in a landscape, as Prudence (see below). Inscribed: *Omne Numen adest.*

A 'beautifull desireable Creature', daughter of Sir Edward Stanley. A 'celebrated Beautie and Courtezane', in her youth she had been 'kept as his Concubine' by the 3rd Earl of Dorset. Aubrey (pp.189–91) wrote a famous description of her 'most lovely and sweet turn'd face, delicate dark-browne hair', her short oval face and the colour of her cheeks: 'just that of the Damaske rose, which is neither too hott nor too pale'.

She married, probably in 1626 and against his mother's wishes, Sir Kenelm Digby, to whom she was a blameless wife. She died on 1 May 1633. Digby mourned her extravagantly and caused her to be commemorated in paint and in sculpture. Van Dyck was commissioned to paint her on her death-bed 'the second day after she was dead' (V. Gabrieli, *Sir Kenelm Digby* (Rome, 1957), pp.246, 248). Digby also conceived, as a further tribute to her and perhaps as a vindication of her reputation, an allegorical portrait, on the scale of life, of which he described the iconography to Bellori (p.261): '. . . as Prudence, sitting in a white dress with a coloured wrap and a jewelled girdle. Under her hand are two white doves, and her other arm is encircled by a serpent. Under her feet is a plinth to which are bound, in the guise of slaves, Deceit with two faces; Anger with furious countenance; meagre Envy with her snaky locks; Profane Love, with eyes bound, wings clipped, arrows scattered and torch extinguished; with other naked figures the size of life. Above is a glory of singing Angels, three of them holding the palm and the wreath above the head of Prudence as a symbol of her victory and triumph over the vices; and the epigram, taken from Juvenal, NULLUM NUMEN ABEST SI SIT PRUDENTIA'.

The best-known life-size version of the design is in the royal collection (Millar, no.179), but it is probably only a contemporary copy. A better version is in the Palazzo Reale, Milan. Flaws in Sir Kenelm Digby's memory may be the reason for discrepancies between Bellori's account

9

and the design as it has come down to us. The likeness of Lady Digby was presumably based on Van Dyck's own earlier portrait of her in a family group, of which the most accessible version is at Welbeck (Glück, 398).

Bellori added that Van Dyck was so pleased with the composition that he also painted a small version which, with the original, was taken to France in the Civil War, perhaps by Sir Kenelm himself. In Cardinal Mazarin's inventory (1661) was (no.1235) a version *faict par Vandeck*, stated to measure 36×29 in (Comte de Cosnac, *Les Richesses du Palais Mazarin* (Paris, 1884), pp.337–8). No.9, formerly in the collection of Thomas Walker and Mr Skinner, and later in the Harvey collection at Rolls Park, passed into the possession of Mrs Gibbs and was sold at Christie's, 29 June 1962 (69). The delicate touch on a small scale, the freer neo-Venetian handling in such passages as the figure of Deceit, and the beauty of tone throughout argue strongly for Van Dyck's authorship. A contemporary (?), but less good, version on the same scale, formerly in the Van Berg collection, was sold at Sotheby's, 25 June 1969 (100). The composition must have been known on the Continent by an early date. The principal figure in a *Vanitas*, attributed to Teniers, in The Hermitage (Inv. no.6551) is surrounded by four of the five putti who appear in Van Dyck's composition (Agnew, 1968, no.43; *Age of Charles I*, no.107).

Private collection

10 François Langlois (1589–1647)

(COLOUR PLATE II, between pages 16 and 17)

Canvas, 104.5×84.5 (41⅛×33¼)   c1634

The sitter, nicknamed 'Ciartres' from Chartres, his birthplace, was a dealer, principally in prints and drawings, an engraver and a publisher of prints. He secured works for Charles I, Buckingham and the Earl of Arundel. He was living in Italy in the 1620s; he was in London in 1625; and in 1634 he settled in Paris as a dealer in books and prints with a shop in the rue S. Jacques. After his death his widow eventually married Pierre II Mariette, whose grandson was Pierre-Jean Mariette.

Langlois was a good musician and he is painted as a Savoyard, playing the *musette*: a small bagpipe, of aristocratic design, which was popular at court in London and in France and was played by professionals of the Hotteterre-Philidor circle and by ladies and gentlemen in pastoral dress.[1] His coat is a cool scarlet, lined with pink; his cloak is a stronger red in tone. The head of a hound is seen in the lower left corner.

The portrait strikes an unusual note in any Van Dyck exhibition. As Carlos van Hasselt has written, Langlois is shown as 'an itinerant journeyman, shepherd and musician, not very different in type from the gypsy fiddlers who roamed about Europe in search of a living . . . The portrait also probably reflects his romantic and sentimental disposition, combined with a sense of humour and self-mockery' (see the writer's invaluable and detailed account of the preparatory drawing, no.71). The bagpiper was a popular figure in Netherlandish art and Van Hasselt has also suggested that Langlois would have become

familiar in the course of his career with the engravings of Stefano della Bella, Stella and Callot – artists with whom he corresponded – and with the genre scenes of the Carracci: with 'the general artistic activity at Rome and Bologna . . . and the world of beggars in the early seventeenth century'.

Formerly said to have been painted in Italy (eg Glück, 160, and Larsen, no.464), it was apparent, when the portrait was exhibited with a large number of Van Dyck's Italian works, that it was out of place among them (*100 Opere di Van Dyck*, Palazzo dell'Accademia, Genoa (1955), no.29); and it is now generally accepted that both painting and drawings are substantially later. The sitter was in London in October 1637, but the tonality and the handling suggest a date c.1634. The clear blue and soft white in the sky are characteristic of the English period. The instrument is a particularly fine passage of still-life painting: subtly painted and ravishing in colour.

The portrait was engraved by Jean Pesne in 1645. It was in the collection of the Marquis de Maisons (d.1677) and passed through a number of French collections before the Revolution; it was in the Duc de Praslin (1793) and Choiseul-Praslin (1808) sales; later in the collections of Hoppner (his sale by Stanley, 9–10 May 1828 (111)); Miss Tait; and William Garnett.

The Viscount Cowdray

[1]*The New Grove Dictionary of Music and Musicians*, ed. S. Sadie (1980), vol.12, 796; *Musical Instruments through the Ages*, ed. A. Baines (1961), p.239.

11 Charles I on Horseback with M. de St Antoine

(FRONT COVER)

Canvas, 368.4×269.9 (145×106¼)

Dated: *1633*.

The King, holding a baton and wearing armour with the ribbon of the Garter, rides towards the spectator on a white horse through a triumphal arch, from the top of which falls a pale green curtain. At the foot of the arch is a shield bearing the Royal Arms. On the right, in attendance on the King and carrying his helmet, is the Seigneur de St Antoine, in red with the ribbon of either Saint-Lazare and Notre-Dame-du-Mont-Carmel or, less likely, Saint-Michel.

The enormous canvas was hung, 'in a great large Carved frame', at the end of the Gallery at St James's (*Van der Doort*, p.226), a position for which it may have been specially painted and where it made a considerable impression. A member of the suite of Marie de' Medici, who lodged at St James's in November 1638, wrote, for instance: 'At one of the ends of this Gallery . . . there is a portrait of the king . . . armed and on horseback, by the Chevalier Van Dyck. And, without exaggeration, in preserving the state of this great monarch, he has so skilfully brought him to life with his brush, that if our eyes alone were to be believed they would boldly assert that the king was alive in this portrait, so vivid is its appearance' (P. de la Serre, *Histoire de l'Entrée de la Reyne Mère . . ., dans la Grande Bretagne* (1639)). The picture made an equally striking impact when, after the Restoration, it hung at

[handwritten:] Artists own sensitive, nervous fluency gives the vast canvas a flickering rather than a swaggering air. All V D's animals look nervous.

1633

Hampton Court: 'In another gallery . . . at the end was K. Charles the First on horseback, that as you enter at the opposite end, you would think it real' (*The Journal of James Yonge* [*1647–1721*], ed. F.N.L. Poynter (1963), p.172).

The pattern for the portrait is one of the principal equestrian designs which had been evolved by Rubens for use on a variety of scales, and with which Van Dyck would have been familiar in his early years. He would not have known, however, at first hand, Rubens's portrait of the Duke of Lerma (painted in 1603 and now in the Prado), which is the first demonstration by Rubens of the design in which a great man, in armour and holding a baton, rides out towards the spectator on a pale horse; but Charles I would have seen the portrait, with members of his suite, when, as Prince of Wales, he had been in Spain in 1623, and memories of the effect it had made, hanging in the lower gallery in the Casa Real de la Ribera in Valladolid, may partly have inspired the commission to Van Dyck ten years later. The advancing white horse was also used by lesser Flemish painters, particularly Jan Bruegel, many times in the early years of the century, on a small scale and in very different contexts. Rubens used the pattern again for the portrait of Marie de' Medici, in *The Triumph at Jülich* in the Medici series, originally intended to hang on the end wall, opposite the entrance, in the gallery for which the series was painted (see F. Huemer, *Corpus Rubenianum*, part XIX, I, pp.21–5, 54).

Van Dyck had used the pattern at least twice in Genoa, for portraits of Cornelis de Wael (Larsen, no.331) and Antonio Giulio Brignole Sale (Glück, 420); but in none of them is there the combination of scale, sheer splendour in the majesty of the sitter and in the way in which he is presented, and totally convincing stagecraft: a combination which is not to be seen again in the work of any other painter working within this convention.

Van Dyck's greatness as an artist, and the quality of this particular composition, are apparent when it is compared with the attempts made to copy it. Copies, in some cases with simplification, were certainly being commissioned in the 1640s and 1650s, but even the better copies (eg at Warwick Castle, Corsham Court, Apsley House or Hampton Court) are uniformly undistinguished and, with the possible exception of the copy at Corsham, lack freshness of touch. Many small copies are recorded; and the composition was used by later painters, normally on a reduced scale, for other sitters (for fuller details on these points, see Millar, no.143). Van Dyck himself used the pattern once more in his portrait of the Marquis of Moncada in the Louvre (Glück, 420).

Every inch of this huge canvas reveals the freshness and fluency of the painter's touch; and the background and accessories are as finely painted as the horse and rider. An impression of spontaneity, of many details being worked out as the painter developed the composition, is created by the *pentimenti* in such details as the outline of the King's thigh, the position of his head and baton, the placing of the bridle and bit and the length of the horse's rear standing leg. The quality of drawing and painting is consistently distinguished throughout the design. Particularly brilliant passages are the superbly drawn stirrup and foot, the fresh and sensitively modelled head of the horse, the sil-very lights which are used to define the play of bone and muscle down the horse's legs, the exceptionally delicate modelling of the King's features with light touches of silver and pink, the liquid handling of the armour, the more softly defined features of St Antoine. The sky, incidentally, was painted up to the completed figure of the King. The light underpaint is clearly seen, for instance, down the far side of the head, down the left shoulder, under the upper part of the right arm, to the left of the Garter ribbon and between the collar and the sky. Perhaps the most remarkable feature of the picture is the harmony of tone and balance of the varied elements in the composition. A quiet, refined poise is the painter's conspicuous achievement on this huge scale, with the gentle, insistent concentration most clearly expressed in the adoring look of the equerry, and conveyed by a gradual intensification in the texture and handling as the eye is led up to the hand, the armour and the collar, and then to the tranquil, reserved face of the King. Even the most lustrous passages of paint and colour do not disturb the equilibrium. On the other hand the picture is a supreme example, on a very big scale, of the artist's ability to convey a sense of movement, which never gets out of hand, within a still and disciplined framework (the same contrast is felt on a smaller scale in, for instance, no.41); a breeze disturbs the curtain and stirs the horse's mane. Van Dyck's arbitrary handling of elements in space can be illustrated by the realization that if the right-hand side of the arch had been drawn down to its foot there would be no room for St Antoine. The fall of curtain serves to cover up this difficulty and to provide a beautiful tonal backcloth for the equerry. The element of illusion is far more profound than it seemed to contemporary admirers of Van Dyck's achievement; and it was characteristically more important for Van Dyck to retain the psychological element and the contrasts in colour on the right of the design than to clarify the position of the column and its base.

The King is seen as the ruler of Great Britain and one of the finest horsemen in Europe;[1] horsemanship, associated with virtue and courage, was an essential element in a prince. The placing of the picture in the Gallery at St James's may have given it added significance at the time. Among the European masterpieces, acquired by the King, which lined the walls of the Gallery, were the twelve Emperors by Titian and the little pictures of Emperors on horseback by Giulio Romano, which, with a number of other representations of imperial figures, had been among the ingredients from which Rubens had evolved this design. The King is also to be seen, therefore, as heir to the imperial tradition as it was illustrated in his own collection, especially by Titian.

No.68 is a preliminary drawing for the composition; see no.69 for a study of the horse (Millar, no.143).

Her Majesty The Queen

[1]The Seigneur de St Antoine, a master in the art of horsemanship, had been sent to England by the King of France in 1603 with a present of horses for the Prince of Wales. He remained in royal service in this country as riding-master and equerry.

12

Fig.37 Daniel Mytens, *Philip Herbert, 4th Earl of Pembroke.*
The Marquess of Salisbury

12 Philip Herbert, 4th Earl of Pembroke (1584–1650)

Canvas, 105.4×83.8 (41½×33)

Half-length, seated, wearing the ribbon of the Garter and holding in his left hand his wand of office as Lord Chamberlain, a post he held from 1626 to 1641.

He and his brother, the 3rd Earl, were among the most cultivated and lavish patrons of the arts and letters. They were 'the Most Noble and Incomparable Pair of Brethren' to whom the First Folio was dedicated. The collection of pictures built up by the 4th Earl was almost entirely dispersed, but Wilton House survives as a monument to enlightened patronage of architects, painters, interior decorators and gardeners. As Earl of Montgomery he was a prominent performer in masques at the court of James I (he performed at least once in the following reign). Good looks and a devotion to field sports had endeared him to James I, but he 'was not strongly built, nor had sufficient ballast to endure a storm', and he eventually deserted the royal cause. Aubrey (pp.225–6) stated that he 'exceedingly loved Painting and Building . . . and was the great Patron to Sir Anthony van Dyck: and had most of his Painting'. Aubrey's claim would be difficult to substantiate – the King and Lord Wharton almost certainly owned more pictures by Van Dyck; but the Earl commissioned the celebrated family group (fig.31), the most magnificent surviving piece from Van Dyck's English period: 'one of the best pieces that ever he drew', in Aubrey's words (Bodleian Library, MS Aubrey, 2, f.34), set into the panelling of 'the great Dining-roome, or Roome of State', at

Wilton, now known as the Double Cube Room.

No.12 was probably painted at about the same period (ie *c.*1634) as the portrait of the Earl in the great picture, or possibly slightly earlier. It is perhaps unusually dry and restrained in quality but makes an interesting contrast with a portrait (fig.37) of the same sitter painted *c.*1625 by Daniel Mytens. The compositions are not dissimilar, but the later portrait has a sheer distinction and a latent sense of movement unattainable by the earlier painter.

The portrait came from Kyre Park, the seat of the Baldwyn-Childe family, who had inherited it from Jonathan Pitts (d.1807); it was acquired from Colnaghi by the Felton Bequest in 1937 (U. Hoff, *European Paintings before Eighteen Hundred*, National Gallery of Victoria (1967), pp.38–9; *Age of Charles I*, no.104; Larsen, no.842).

Felton Bequest, National Gallery of Victoria, 1937

13 Henry Percy, 9th Earl of Northumberland (1564–1632)

Canvas, 137.2×119.4 (54×47)

Inscribed later: *Henry Earl of/Northumberland*

Three-quarter-length, seated at a table on which he rests his right elbow; his head is supported on his right hand. By his elbow is a clock and a paper on which is a passage in Latin and a drawing of a mathematical experiment. He wears a robe richly laced with gold.

The Earl had been arrested for complicity in the Gunpowder Plot, although he pleaded that 'the course of his

13

life, unambitious and given to private pleasures, such as gardening, building, &c.', argued powerfully for his innocence. He was fined £30,000 by the Court of Star Chamber and imprisoned in the Tower, 1605–21, but he carried out experiments with his fellow-prisoner, Raleigh, and pursued his scholarly interests, especially in the field of mathematics in which he was a notable patron. He built up a magnificent library.

The Earl died on 5 November 1632 and the portrait was painted posthumously for his son, the 10th Earl (see no.24). Van Dyck was called upon on a number of occasions to paint posthumous portraits for family galleries (he did two, for instance, for the King and one for the Earl of Pembroke). Symonds saw at Northumberland House on 27 December 1652 one such ancestral portrait 'Done by helpe of another Picture after the party was dead' as well as no.13: 'Another of his Ancestors an old man sitting in a Gowne & leaning on a Table, done by an old picture'.[1]

The mood and the (rather uncomfortable) posture are melancholy and reflective and the costume emphasizes the sitter's scholarly nature. The quality of the handling is very fresh throughout – there is a *pentimento* in the outline of the sitter's right hand – and the portrait is remarkably thoughtful and sensitive considering that it was based on 'another Picture', which may have been a miniature. Characteristically, the still life is painted with a particularly fresh touch (Collins Baker, *Petworth*, p.29, no.223).

HM Treasury and the National Trust, Egremont Collection, Petworth

[1]The Northumberland pictures, which are today to be seen at Petworth, had passed to the 10th Earl's granddaughter, the Duchess of Somerset, whose daughter married Sir William Wyndham, ancestor of the Lords Egremont and Leconfield.

14 William Laud (1573–1645), Archbishop of Canterbury

(COLOUR PLATE III, between pages 16 and 17)

Canvas, 121.6×97.2 (47⅞×38¼)

Three-quarter-length, in rochet and chimere, resting his right arm on a column; a red and gold curtain behind.

The son of a Reading draper, educated at Oxford, he owed his advancement to the patronage of the Duke of Buckingham, and became successively Bishop of St David's, 1621, Bath and Wells, 1626, and London, 1628, and, in 1633, Archbishop of Canterbury. He was a sound and practical administrator of passionate integrity, a devoted servant of the King, dedicated unswervingly to enforcing uniformity in worship in the English Church. He aroused intense antagonism, was impeached in December 1640, imprisoned in the Tower and beheaded in 1645. A fine Hebrew scholar, he collected Oriental manuscripts which he presented to his old University; he has been described as the greatest Chancellor the University has ever had. The Canterbury Quadrangle at St John's was built at his expense. He also put in hand with characteristic energy the restoration of St Paul's.

The Archbishop probably sat to Van Dyck in 1635. Recent cleaning and restoration of no.14 has confirmed the belief that it is the finest extant version of the portrait, although little is known of its provenance before it appeared at Christie's on 30 January 1920 (267), when it was bought by Charles Ricketts and C. H. Shannon. It was part of the Shannon Bequest to the Fitzwilliam Museum in 1937.

The portrait is undocumented and it has to be pointed out that there is no evidence for Laud's giving a commission to Van Dyck. Nor, if Laud had commissioned a portrait to hang in Lambeth Palace, is there evidence that this was the one painted for the purpose. Professor Michael Jaffé has, however, properly established the pre-eminent importance of the portrait. He has pointed to its probable dependence, in pattern, on the great full-length of Scaglia (no.17), to such particularly fine passages as the nervous painting of the hands, and the piercing glance, and to the vigorous quality and freshness which characterize the entire canvas (there are *pentimenti* in the ruff and in the outline of the sitter's left arm). Professor Jaffé, in discussing many copies and derivations, is right to amend the views of Goodison (1960), Piper (1963) and Ingamells (1981) and to put into their correct order such inferior, if better known, copies as those at Wentworth Woodhouse, Lambeth Palace and The Hermitage. One of the better copies (sold at Christie's, 29–30 July 1971 (232)) is the one painted for Clarendon, who wrote a celebrated character-study of the Archbishop; another good version was formerly at Bramshill.

I am very much indebted to Professor Jaffé for allowing me to read, before publication, his article, 'Van Dyck Studies I: The Portrait of Archbishop Laud', to be published in *The Burlington Magazine*.

Fitzwilliam Museum, Cambridge

15

15 Thomas Wentworth, 1st Earl of Strafford (1593–1641)

Canvas, 229.9×142.9 (90½×56¼)

Full-length, standing, in armour with crimson breeches; his plumed helmet is on a ledge beside him. In his left hand he holds a baton and his right he rests on the head of a large Irish wolfhound.

Member of Parliament, in opposition to the Crown, 1614–29. He became an ardent supporter of the King, as, principally, Lord President of the Council of the North, 1628–41, Lord Deputy General, and later Lord Lieutenant, of Ireland. His most recent and affectionate biographer writes that from a mass of evidence 'there emerges the image of a strong and resolute man, of great practical ability, of powerful intellect, of tireless energy; over-confident in his own opinions, over-certain of his own rectitude; not always scrupulous in the pursuit of public power and personal advantage; but a man of generous vision and unswerving loyalty' (C. V. Wedgwood, *Thomas Wentworth First Earl of Strafford A Revaluation* (1961), p.397).

He was one of Van Dyck's most sensitive patrons and it is significant that all the three portrait-patterns that Van Dyck evolved for him were derived from pictures by Titian which were then in London. This full-length was inspired by the portrait of Charles V with a hound, now in the Prado (Wethey, vol.II, no.20) but then in the Bear Gallery at Whitehall. It obviously commemorated Wentworth's appointment in January 1632 as Lord Deputy General of Ireland. Charles V's hound was described by Van der Doort (p.4) as 'a bigg white irish dogg' and no.15 may have been painted on the eve of Wentworth's departure for Dublin in July 1633.[1] On the other hand it may be the portrait, 'the first originall of my Picture at large', which the sitter instructed his agent, in a letter dated 5 September 1636, to send down to Wentworth Woodhouse from London. As late as 15 November 1636 'that great picture wch is for Woodhouse', designed for 'one of the places in the Gallery there', had not left London. It was certainly that picture from which Hoskins was instructed to make copies in miniature; 'and desire Sr Anthony from me to help him with his direction'. There are beautifully fluent passages, especially in the hound and the boots. The original drawn outline of the right leg is clearly visible with the heavy paint, modelling the boot, swept over it. Many copies and derivations, principally as three-quarter-lengths, are recorded (R.A., 1953–4, no.148).

Trustees of the Rt Hon Olive, Countess Fitzwilliam's Chattels Settlement. Lent by kind permission of Lady Juliet de Chair

[1]The group of Strafford family portraits, which were formerly at Wentworth Woodhouse, passed as heirlooms to Lady Anne Wentworth (see no.32), to her third son and ultimately to the 2nd Marquess of Rockingham, whose sister married the 3rd Earl Fitzwilliam.

16 William Feilding, 1st Earl of Denbigh (c.1582–1643)

c. 1633

(COLOUR PLATE IV, between pages 16 and 17)

Canvas, 247.5×148.5 (97½×58½)

Full-length, in a landscape, wearing a pink silk Hindu or Indian jacket and pyjamas with a narrow gold stripe. He carries a flint-lock fowling-piece, probably of French or Flemish origin, and makes a gesture of mild surprise as an Oriental servant, in a tunic of deep gold and a turban, points to a parrot perched in a palm tree.

Marriage with the Duke of Buckingham's sister brought Denbigh favour at court. Master of the Great Wardrobe, 1622, and a member of the Prince of Wales's suite on the visit to the Spanish court – the 'Spanish Marriage Venture' – in 1623. In the Civil War he fought for the King 'with unwearied pains and exact submission to discipline and order' as a volunteer in Prince Rupert's Troop, and he died of wounds received in the attack on Birmingham, 8 April 1643 (Clarendon, vol.III, p.20).

In August 1633 he returned from a journey or embassy to the Shah of Persia and the Great Mogul in India. He had set out in 1631 in order, in his own words, 'to better my understanding'. Van Dyck's portrait was obviously commissioned to commemorate this experience. The Earl had brought back with him pieces of 'Mesopotamia cloth' and 'an old pagan coat', and the costume he wears is of a type worn at that date by Europeans in India.

The portrait, probably painted soon after the Earl's return, may have been commissioned by, or given to, the Marquess of Hamilton (no.60) who had married Denbigh's daughter. In inventories (in the possession of the present Duke) of Hamilton's pictures it appears as: 'Vendick My Lorde Denbeigh & Jacke' and as 'One peice

Fig.38 Marcus Gheeraerts, *Thomas Lee.* The Trustees of the Tate Gallery

56

16 (detail)

of my lords denbighs at length, with a fowlinge peece in his hande, and a Blackamore by him of S.' Anthony: Van-dyke'. It remained in the Hamilton collection until 1919; subsequently, until 1938, at Newnham Paddox, it was acquired by Count Antoine Seilern and presented by him to the National Gallery in 1945.

In the composition Van Dyck was as ambitious – and successful – in attempting to plant a full-length figure in a landscape as he was in the famous portrait of the King in the hunting-field (fig.18); but in this instance the sitter strides – or lurches – forward towards the spectator and through the landscape which is no longer the decorative backcloth that it was, for example, in Mytens's *Earl of Holland* (fig.21) or Gheeraerts's *Captain Thomas Lee* (fig.38). As a composition, and as a superb display of brilliant drawing and richly handled paint, especially in the foreground and in the heads and the whites, it is one of Van Dyck's most beautiful and important English portraits, no less so for being something of an 'exotic' among his more conventional images. Martin, in a very full treatment of the picture (*Catalogue*, pp.52–5), points to *pentimenti* in the upper part of the Earl's left leg; in traces of a wide-brimmed castor in his left hand; and in the outline of his left arm. There is a characteristic silhouetting of the legs in opaque paint. A number of copies or derivations are recorded.

The Trustees of the National Gallery

17 Cesare Alessandro Scaglia, Abbé of Stafforda and Mandanici (d.1641)

Canvas, 204.5 × 124.5 (80½ × 49)

Full-length, in black, leaning with his right arm on a ledge; a chair and curtain on the right.

A diplomat in the service of the Dukes of Savoy. He was ambassador in Rome, 1614–23, and to Paris, 1625–7; and in addition undertook a number of special missions, working always in the pro-English and pro-Spanish interests. He was in London, 1631–2. After retirement he remained in contact with Philip IV, and in Brussels in 1634 he was in the confidence of Prince Thomas of Savoy, Captain-General of the Spanish troops in the Netherlands. In 1639 he moved to Antwerp. He had for many years known the leading Flemish painters; and towards the end of his life he was employed to negotiate between Balthazar Gerbier, Rubens and Jordaens for the series of paintings for the decoration of the Queen's Bedchamber at Greenwich. He was regarded as 'having good skill in handling such mercenary men'.

From the spring of 1634 until some time in 1635 Van Dyck was back in the Spanish Netherlands, working in Antwerp and Brussels. In this comparatively short period he produced a remarkable number of pictures, including portraits of members of the court at Brussels. The portrait of Scaglia in particular is one of the finest he ever produced, with its combination of splendour and restraint, of monumentality and latent movement. Characteristic of the period are the fresh touch throughout and the refined

handling and texture. The aura round the head marks the area on which Van Dyck worked when actually painting the head, before figure, accessories and background had been tackled. The Abbé also commissioned from Van Dyck the painting in the National Gallery in which he is seen in adoration of the Virgin and Child (the above is largely based on Christopher Brown's number (2) in the series, *Painting in Focus*, published by the National Gallery: 'The Abbé Scaglia adoring the Virgin and Child').

Van Dyck's design was perhaps influenced by Titian's three-quarter-length of Benedetto Varchi (fig.39) in which the sitter, in black, leans against just such a column. Van Dyck's drawing of the Abbé, full-length but seated (Vey, no.192), may indicate that he first intended, however, to paint him sitting by a table. The pattern of the final portrait was used by Van den Enden in the *Iconography*; and it may have been through this plate that the design became known in England. Emanuel de Critz used it, for example, in 1657, for his portrait of Sir John Maynard at Helmingham Hall. A good second version of no.17 is in Antwerp (no.405).

No.17 was in the Baring collection by 1815, when Sir Thomas Baring lent it to the British Institution (11); sold to R. S. Holford before 1851; Holford sale, Christie's, 17 May 1928 (61).

The Viscount Camrose

Fig.39 Titian, *Benedetto Varchi*. Kunsthistorisches Museum, Vienna

58

17

1635

18 The Three eldest Children of Charles I

Canvas, 153.7×156.8 (60½×61¾)

A full-length group, the two eldest children on a reddish carpet (on which lie some pink roses), against a green curtain. Charles, Prince of Wales, stands on the left in a lace cap and a pale scarlet frock decorated with silvery-grey lace and ribbons, resting his hand on a large red-brown spaniel; Mary, Princess Royal, in white with pink bows; James, Duke of York, in a lace cap and a blue doublet and frock, clasping an apple.[1]

Painted in 1635 to be sent by the Queen to her elder sister, Christina, Duchess of Savoy, who sent portraits of her own children to London in return. In an undated letter

(probably written in July) the Queen told her sister that in a week's time she would send *'les pourtraicts des mes enfans'*; she added that they would have been dispatched earlier, but *'ma fille n'a jamais voulu avoir la pasiance de les leser achever tel qu'il est je le vous envoye j'en feray faire une autre pour elle qui sera mieux'*. Later, probably in the autumn, when the picture had still not been dispatched, she told the Duchess that it would be sent within a week; but in a letter dated 29 November Benoît Cize, the ambassador from Savoy to London, told his master that the Queen had shown him *'Les Portraits des messeigneurs les Princes les enfans'* destined for the Duchess. The Queen told Cize that the King was displeased with (*'faché contre'*) Van Dyck, apparently for having painted them in such childish dress (*'po' ne leur avoir mis leur Tablié comme on accoustume aux petit enfans*').[2] It was probably partly to correct this error that Van Dyck was commissioned to paint for the Queen the slightly later group of her children (Millar, no.151; now to be seen in the exhibition, *Kings & Queens*, The Queen's Gallery (1982–4), no.34).

As was to be expected, in carrying out a commission of such importance, Van Dyck produced one of his most ravishing compositions and possibly the most enchanting study of childhood in his career. Sir Lionel Cust went so far as to describe it as 'perhaps the most beautiful piece of child-portraiture in the world'. A delicate touch and an exquisite, almost Watteau-like, range of colour are sustained right across the canvas and are completely in tune with the sensitive delineation of the characters and features. Of a particularly transparent beauty are such passages as the lace on the Prince of Wales's costume, the pattern on the Princess's costume, the watercolour texture of the thread round her left wrist and the floating of the aprons, with their lace edges, over the frocks of the two youngest children. It is more subtly painted throughout than the later group of the three children and noticeably different in texture from the large group painted two years later (no.26).

Because it immediately entered the collection of the Duke of Savoy the composition was comparatively little known and, in contrast with the two other groups of the children, was not extensively copied or plagiarized. Copies of the head of the Duke of York are recorded (*100 Opere di Van Dyck*, Palazzo dell'Accademia, Genoa (1955), no.91).

Galleria Sabauda, Turin

[1]Herrick, in the *Poet's good wishes* for the little Duke of York, had expressed the hope that he would grow 'Like t'a Rose of *Jericho*'; and that the tread of his soft foot would produce gardens and meadows set with the rose and the violet. The apple, presumably as a symbol of fruitfulness, is held in the same way in the miniature of a girl by Isaac Oliver (1590) in the Victoria and Albert Museum.

[2]H. Ferrero, *Lettres de Henriette-Marie de France à sa sœur Christina Duchesse de Savoie* (Turin, 1881), pp.40, 43; Mazzo-Lettere Ministri Inghilterra, Archivio di Stato, Turin.

Not available for exhibition.

19 Elizabeth Stuart, Lady Maltravers and later Countess of Arundel (d.1674)

Canvas, 74.3 × 59 (29¼ × 23¼)

On the back of the original canvas are two contemporary inscriptions, the first written under a cross: *I Elizabeth Loueis:/Arrundell & Surrey/I leave this my picture to my/Lord & his Ayres/1649*; and: *this drawne by S* *r*/*Antony vandike In/1635*.

Head and shoulders to the left in a white dress with a fur across her right shoulder.

The sitter was a daughter of the Duke of Lennox and sister of nos.44, 48 and 61; in 1626 she had married, against the wishes of the King, Lord Maltravers, eldest surviving son of the Earl of Arundel.

The inscription came to light when the portrait was restored in 1964. Something of the subtlety of the portrait

19

had doubtless been lost in earlier restorations, but much survives of the original delicacy of touch and refinement of colour, particularly in the silvers and pinks in the flesh. There are slight *pentimenti* in the position of the drops from the left ear. The format is unusual in Van Dyck's *œuvre* and may reflect the influence of Cornelius Johnson; in one or two other small female portraits the same influence can be detected.

The portrait passed by descent to the Greystoke branch of the family, perhaps through the sitter's fourth son, Charles Howard of Greystoke. A copy is at Arundel and the type was used for the portrait of the Countess in the late seventeenth-century group of portrait-miniatures also at Arundel (Hervey, p.524; O. Millar, 'Notes on British Art 2', *Apollo* (January, 1965), pp.1–2; Agnew, 1968, no.47; Larsen, no.818).

Stafford Howard, Esq

20 Henry Danvers, Earl of Danby (1573–1644)

Canvas, 223×130.6 (87¾×51⅜)

Full-length, standing to the left front, in Garter robes. He rests his right hand on a table on which is the hat of the Order. The table-cloth and curtain behind are of the same rich fabric, patterned in gold and green.

A distinguished soldier who had in his youth been a page to Sir Philip Sidney. Served in the Low Countries under Prince Maurice of Orange and in Ireland with Essex. He and his brother murdered Henry Long at Corsham in 1594 and, until they were pardoned four years later, Henry Danvers served, with conspicuous bravery, in the armies of Henry IV of France (the formidable scar near his left eye can already be seen in a much earlier portrait at Woburn Abbey). Lord President of Munster, 1607–15, and later Governor of Guernsey. 'Tall and spare; Temperate; sedate and solid; a very great favourite of Prince Henry . . . a great Improver of his Estate . . . A great Oeconomist . . . All his servants were sober and wise in their respective places' (Aubrey, p.171). He gave to Oxford University the land and the endowment for the Botanic or Physic Garden; and he commissioned Nicholas Stone to make the three gateways for it and to design for him a new house at Cornbury Park of which he had been granted the Rangership in 1617: it has been described as 'one of the earliest attempts to design a classical country house front in England' (Jennifer Sherwood in *The Buildings of Britain: Oxfordshire* (1974), p.553).

He was prominent among the connoisseurs at the court of James I and was interested in the work of Rubens. In 1623 he had sent a commission for a *Self-portrait* which he could present to the Prince of Wales, for his gallery at St James's, and which happily survives at Windsor.

Created a Knight of the Garter in November 1633, he was installed with the Earl of Morton, and his 'gravity of habit', according to Aubrey (pp.171–2) 'got the advantage', in the eyes of the judicious, of his more extravagantly adorned companion. The broad, but very fluent, handling in the portrait suggests that no.20 was painted at a rather later date (a hurried preliminary drawing, at three-quarter-length, is in the British Museum (Vey, no.212)). With its rich atmosphere and dramatic tensions, and in the complete harmony between head and figure, it is one of Van Dyck's greatest English portraits; the superbly posed figure is full of movement, principally in the pull of the left arm and hand against the direction of the gesture of the right hand, the extended right arm and the thrust of the right leg. The soft and shimmering quality in such passages as the whites and soft golds in the costume and the sword makes an interesting contrast with the hardness of such passages in, for instance, many of the portraits from Lord Wharton's gallery; and they are set off by the soft scarlet and blue of the Garter robes.

It is the only full-length of a Garter Knight in Van Dyck's œuvre. Among a very small number of precedents the most important are Gheeraerts's *Sir Henry Lee* of 1602 and Cornelius Johnson's *Earl of Mulgrave*, c.1620 (fig.40), at Cranford Hall. Van Dyck's example stimulated an increased number of such portraits after the Restoration,

principally from Lely, whose full-length designs for Garter Knights were influenced by his predecessor. Copies are recorded, eg at Dunham Massey, and, with variations, at Christie's, 22 November 1974 (105).

The portrait passed as an heirloom to Danby's nephew, John Danvers, and was presented by his son, Sir Joseph Danvers, to Sir Robert Walpole. It was subsequently among the pictures acquired by Catherine the Great with the Walpole collection in 1779 (Varshavskaya, p.127, no.24).

The Hermitage, Leningrad

Fig.40 Cornelius Johnson, *Edmund Sheffield, 1st Earl of Mulgrave*. Sir John Robinson

20

c 1635-6

21 Thomas Howard, 2nd Earl of Arundel (1585–1646), with his grandson Thomas, later 5th Duke of Norfolk (1627–77)

Canvas, 145.4 × 121.9 (57¼ × 48)

Three-quarter-lengths in a landscape with a curtain of deep gold falling down behind the figures. The Earl, in armour with the badge of the Garter and with the Earl Marshal's baton in his right hand, rests his left hand on the shoulder of his grandson, dressed in pink, who holds a paper in his right hand.

The Earl, who had become a Protestant, was restored in 1621 to the office of Earl Marshal. He was to preside, as Lord High Steward, at the trial of Strafford. Justly celebrated in the history of collecting and connoisseurship, Arundel built up a superb collection of pictures, drawings and marbles at Arundel House. He was also a discerning patron of contemporary artists and craftsmen: 'one that Loved and favored all artes and artists in a great measure, and was the bringer of them in to Englande'. His grandson, the eldest son of Lord and Lady Maltravers (no.19), fell into 'a distemper of the brain' in Padua in 1645, but was restored to the Dukedom of Norfolk in 1660.

Painted, probably *c.* 1635–6, for the Earl. In November 1636 he wrote to William Petty in Rome that he was sending out 'a Picture of my owne and my little Tom bye me; and desire it may be done at Florence in marble *Basso relievo*, to try a yonge Sculptor there whoe is said to be *valente Huomo*, Francesco hath his name. I could wish Cavaliere Bernino, or Fra[ncesco Fi]amengo, might doe another of the [sam]e'.

Appropriately, in the service of a patron to whom he owed so much, Van Dyck produced one of his most splendid works, rich in handling and beautiful in the contrast between the silvery tones of hair and armour and the predominant cool reds and golds in costume and curtains. The armour is a particularly fine area of glowing baroque handling, the lights reflecting at one point the grandson's pink jacket. The heads are fully and carefully modelled. The surface gains in liveliness from such passages as the quick, nervous drawing of the shadows between the Earl's fingers on the boy's shoulder. The baton, incidentally, was painted directly over the armour. The psychological contrast between the two sitters is most engaging.

A number of copies and derivations are recorded, including, in the Clarendon collection, a full-length figure of the Earl by himself. A copy, inscribed later – and wrongly – as by Dobson was sold at Christie's, 27 November 1959 (109). A version of the head of the Earl, in a painted oval, is at Arundel, and the type was etched in this format in London in 1639 by Hollar (P.1351), who also used the type in the same year in his etched equestrian portrait of his patron (P.1352). In some of the copies the sheet of paper held by 'little Tom' contains sketches, as in no.59, of the armorial animals of the family.

The compositional type, in which a great man (or woman) is accompanied by a small servant or relation, is Venetian in origin (see for instance Titian's *Laura dei Dianti* or *Guidobaldo II della Rovere*, Wethey, vol.II, nos.24 and 91); and in England it was taken up, in imitation of

Van Dyck, by such painters as Walker, Dobson and Lely (Hervey, pp.23–4, 391, 478; R.A., 1953–4, no.136; Agnew, 1968, no.45).

His Grace the Duke of Norfolk, CB, CBE, MC, DL

22 Charles I (1600–49) in three Positions

Canvas, 84.5 × 99.7 (33¼ × 39¼)   1635/6

The head of the King is seen in profile, full face, and facing the left front, dressed respectively in black, scarlet and cold crimson with the ribbon and star of the Garter.

The most famous of Van Dyck's representations of his patron: a profound and discerning analysis of the King's personality, expressions and bone structure. It was painted so that Gianlorenzo Bernini could carve a marble bust of the King. He had been authorized to do so by Pope Urban VIII at a time when hopes were entertained in Rome that the King might lead England back into the Catholic fold. Friendship between the Vatican and Whitehall was strengthened by the gift of pictures and works of art between the two courts, and Van Dyck painted for the Pope's nephew, Cardinal Barberini, a particularly beautiful portrait of the Queen (*Age of Charles I*, no.88, reproduced (wrongly captioned) on p.62). The commission to Bernini had apparently come from the Queen, and she eventually rewarded the sculptor with a diamond valued at 4000 *scudi*.

In theory it would not have been necessary for Van Dyck to produce so complete a composition. Bernini would only have needed a sketch of the King's head in three positions on a plain canvas, such as Kneller was to provide for Rysbrack in preparation for a bust of the Earl of Winchilsea and Nottingham (N.P.G., no.3910). Van Dyck was probably encouraged to produce a complete picture partly by the inspiration of Lotto's famous triple portrait of a jeweller (now in Vienna) which then hung at Whitehall with an attribution to Titian (*Van der Doort*, p.20) and partly, perhaps, by the realization that his reputation in artistic circles in Rome would rest on this particular portrait of his patron. There is an obvious parallel with Philippe de Champaigne's study (in the National Gallery) of the head of Cardinal Richelieu in three positions, also perhaps painted to be sent to Bernini's studio.

The colour scheme is of exceptional beauty, especially in the contrast between the pale blue Garter ribbon and the three different costumes. The faces are modelled with a delicacy and a restrained use of pigment which are reminiscent of the finest heads of the second Flemish period; and to contrast the broken blues and greys in the sky with the warm sienna shadows in the heads was also one of Van Dyck's most characteristic Flemish practices. The hairs are drawn with a very fine and nervous touch and in medium of the consistency of watercolour.

Work on the canvas was probably begun in the second half of 1635; and the portrait was dispatched to Rome in the following spring. The bust was sent from Rome, under special escort, in April 1637, after it had been on public exhibition in Rome, and was presented to the King and

65

1635/6

Queen at Oatlands on 17 July 1637. It was enthusiastically received: universally admired 'nott only for the exquisitenesse of the worke but the likenesse and nere resemblance it had to the King's countenance'. The Queen's immediate reaction was to commission a companion bust of herself (see nos.53 and 54, and R. W. Lightbown, 'The journey of the Bernini bust of Charles I to England', *The Connoisseur*, vol.169 (1968), pp.217–20). Bernini's bust was destroyed in the fire at Whitehall Palace in 1698. Traditionally, something of its appearance is thought to be recorded in a marble bust of the King at Windsor; but it has been suggested recently that the bust does not reproduce the Bernini but is a copy after François Dieussart and that he, in his bust of the King (dated 1636) at Arundel may also have been inspired to some extent by Van Dyck's triple portrait (C. Avery, 'François Dieussart (*c*.1600–61), Portrait Sculptor to the Courts of Northern Europe', *Victoria & Albert Museum Yearbook*, vol.IV (1974), pp.65–70; M. Vickers, 'Rupert of the Rhine', *Apollo*, vol.CVII (1978), pp.161–9).

The triple portrait remained in the hands of Bernini's descendants, was bought from the Palazzo Bernini in 1802 and put up for sale at Christie's in 1804. It was eventually secured in 1822 by George IV for 1000 guineas from William Wells. The standard of the many recorded copies is almost invariably depressing. A very early English imitation is a triple portrait of the 8th Earl of Derby(?) which was formerly at Ashburnham Place and may have been based on a single head by Hanneman.

Van Dyck himself used the central head again for a three-quarter-length of the King in armour of which the finest version is at Arundel (Glück, no.392). John Evelyn recorded (*Numismata* (1697), p.201) a tradition that Bernini, on first seeing Van Dyck's portrait, had been struck by 'something of funest and unhappy, which the Countenance of that Excellent Prince foreboded' (Millar, no.146).

Her Majesty The Queen

66

23 Thomas Wentworth, 1st Earl of Strafford (1593–1641)

Canvas, 134 × 109.2 (52¾ × 43)

Three-quarter-length in armour, standing, and, with his right hand, pointing to the right. In his left hand, near his helmet, he holds a baton. In the background, apparently near the sea-shore, is an encampment of cavalry.

For the sitter, see no.15. Wentworth returned to London from Dublin early in June 1636. He was back in Dublin by the end of November. In the intervening months he sat to Van Dyck for a new portrait. On 15 November he wrote to his agent, William Raylton, about the two portraits 'wch weare last drawn now at my being at Eltam; the shortt one is for my Ladye of Carlile, and this you must see to be carefully sett to the frame wch I appointed for itt, and soe lett it stande with Sr Anthonye till you have waited upon her Lap and knowen her pleasure wher shee will have it delivered'. The portrait presumably passed on the death of Lady Carlisle in 1660 to her brother, the Earl of Northumberland. It was not seen by Symonds at Northumberland House in December 1652, but it is listed in the Northumberland inventory of 1671. Raylton was also told not to forget that Lady Carlisle had promised 'her picture allsoe wch may be sent me wth the rest into Irelande': a reference to the full-length still in the Wentworth Woodhouse collection (R.A., 1953–4, no.161).

As for the other portrait: 'The other at lengthe is for my Lo. Newcastle this I would have you to take home to you and in summer . . . take a course that this may be delivered at Wellbecke'. It is still at Welbeck (Glück, no.436). The two portraits are equally fine in quality and Van Dyck designed (fig.41) a special background for the full-length. It would be difficult to establish which was painted first. Perhaps the head – the 'bent and ill-favoured brow' which the sitter himself joked about – and the hands – those hands which the Queen described as the most beautiful in the world – are more spontaneously, if perhaps less solidly, painted in the smaller portrait; the armour is also very freely painted, with brilliant liquid lights. Strafford, giving instructions about the version for Newcastle, specifically asked Raylton to 'minde Sr Anthonye that he will take good paines upon the perfecting of this picture wth his owne pensell'. This is proof that in such a commission, working for a powerful, discerning and demanding patron, Van Dyck would paint two versions of a portrait (the letters in the Wentworth Woodhouse Muniments in Sheffield City Libraries are quoted

Fig.41 *Thomas Wentworth, 1st Earl of Strafford* (detail). Lady Anne Cavendish-Bentinck

23

by kind permission of the Trustees of the Fitzwilliam Estates and the Director of the Libraries).

The posture in the full-length is loosely based on the principal figure in Titian's *Allocution of Alfonso d'Avalos*, now in the Prado (Wethey, vol.II, no.10) but at that time hanging in the First Privy Lodging Room at Whitehall (*Van der Doort*, p.15), where Northumberland, Newcastle and Strafford would frequently have admired it.

A great many copies of the portrait on the smaller scale are recorded. Strafford considered that whereas he was prepared to pay £30 for the original 'halfe pictures' and £50 for 'thos at length', the painter would have to be content with £20 for a copy of the smaller portrait, 'especially taking soe many from him at once and in a deade time allsoe'. The design was also disseminated through Hollar's plate of 1640 (P. no.1508; R.A., *British Portraits*, 1956–7, no.75; Agnew, 1968, no.48).

HM Treasury and the National Trust, Egremont Collection, Petworth

24 Algernon Percy, 10th Earl of Northumberland (1602–68)

Canvas, 72.7×136.5 (28⅝×53¾)

Half-length, in armour with the ribbon of the Garter, holding a baton of command in his right hand and resting his left hand on the fluke of an anchor; a naval engagement in the background.

Created a Knight of the Garter in May 1635, the Earl was appointed *Custos Maris*, Captain-General and Governor of the Fleet, 23 March 1636, and again, during pleasure, 20 March 1638, and Lord High Admiral of England, 13 April 1638. 'A gracefull young man, of great sobriety and regularity, and in all kinds promising and hopefull to be an eminent ornament to the Crown' (Warwick, p.117). He

wielded great territorial influence and was capable and honest; but he increasingly disliked the King's policies and eventually refused the summons to York at the outbreak of the Civil War and was discharged from office. Clarendon described him as the proudest man alive.

He was a distinguished collector of pictures and one of Van Dyck's most generous patrons. Payments to Van Dyck are recorded in his accounts: for example, £200 in the year ending 15 January 1636 and £50 in the year ending 16 January 1640 (see *Burl. Mag.*, vol.XCVII (1955), pp.255–6); and the inventory drawn up in 1671 by Symon Stone of the Northumberland pictures includes seventeen originals and four copies. The Earl himself may only have sat once to Van Dyck and the 'type' was probably first used in the family group (now at Petworth), painted before the death of Lady Northumberland on 6 December 1637 (Collins Baker, *Petworth*, p.30, no.289). Van Dyck used the type in both the portraits (see also no.25) which allude so positively to Northumberland's naval commands. No.24 was noticed by Richard Symonds at Northumberland House when Symon Stone showed him the pictures there on 27 December 1652: 'halfe figure holding upon an anchor, & Shipps in prospective' (British Library, Egerton MS 1636, f.92). It is perhaps of finer quality than the full-length. The sea-fight is fresh and liquid in touch and the drawing throughout is spontaneous. The design was obviously ingeniously worked out to fit a special position, presumably over a mantelpiece, in an interior; a copy is at Penshurst. Its influence is obvious in a portrait, perhaps by Robert Walker, of Richard Deane in the National Maritime Museum; and the head was one of the two portraits engraved after Van Dyck by John Payne (d. *c.*1640; Corbett and Norton, p.16; R.A., 1953–4, no.436; Agnew, 1968, no.51; *Age of Charles I*, no.102).

The Duke of Northumberland

1637

26

25 Algernon Percy, 10th Earl of Northumberland (1602–68)

Canvas, 215.9×127 (85×50)

Full-length, wearing the ribbon of the Garter over his breastplate, in a golden-buff doublet and deep crimson breeches with a blue knot at his knee, all richly laced with gold, resting his right arm on an anchor and holding a baton in his right hand; a naval engagement in the background.

See no.24. The naval action and the head of the sitter, the two elements which are common to both portraits of the Earl, are perhaps more lightly painted than they are in the smaller portrait, which indicates that the full-length, one of Van Dyck's most magnificent designs, was painted slightly later; but the costume and accessories are very freshly painted and the handling is of fine quality throughout the design. A characteristic of the painter's English portraits, especially towards the end of his life, is the use of opaque areas of an Indian red tone to define the outlines of passages such as the hands.

The portrait, which was much copied (a good early copy is at Syon, for example) was given by Northumber-land to his daughter Elizabeth at the time of her marriage to Lord Capel in 1652, and was subsequently at Cassiobury. It was acquired privately from the Earl of Essex at the end of the last century by the 8th Duke of Northumberland. The portrait, which Reynolds must have known well, was the inspiration for his portrait of Lord Rodney which was painted in 1788–9 for the Prince of Wales.

The Duke of Northumberland

26 The Five eldest Children of Charles I

Canvas, 163.2×198.8 (64¼×78¼)

Inscribed, perhaps in the hand of the artist, with the names and ages of the children and: *Antony van dyck Eques Fecit,/1637.*

A full-length group in front of a green curtain and, on the right, a table, covered with a red cloth, on which are a gold jug and a chased dish with fruit. The eldest child, Charles, Prince of Wales (born 29 May 1630), stands, in red, with his left hand on the head of a mastiff. On the left Mary, Princess Royal (born 4 November 1631), stands, in a white dress with apron and leading-strings, beside James,

71

Duke of York (born 14 October 1633), who is still unbreeched and wears an orange petticoat. On the right Princess Elizabeth (born 28 December 1635), in blue with a lace cap, nurses Princess Anne (born 17 March 1637) who lies on a red chair and a pale crimson wrap. A small King Charles spaniel crouches at the foot of the chair.

Painted for Charles I. In the 'Memoire' of pictures which he had painted for him, Van Dyck asked the King £200 for 'Le Prince Carles avecq le ducq de Jarc Princesse Maria. P^sse Elisabet Pr Anna', but the price was halved (Hookham Carpenter, pp.66–8). In a 'blue and carved guilded frame' the picture was placed above the table in the King's Breakfast Chamber in Whitehall (*Van der Doort*, p.35). The group may have been given by James II to the Countess of Dorchester, but it was bought back by George III in 1765.

The latest of Van Dyck's three groups of the royal children (see no.18) and the most ambitious of all his portraits of children, a genre in which he had excelled since his years in Genoa. Sketches in chalk survive for the figure of the Prince of Wales (Royal Library, no.13018; Vey, no.238) and for the Duke of York (no.75). There is also a study in oil (no.27) for the two smallest sitters.

The group is one of Van Dyck's most carefully thought-out designs, with the younger children grouped in a semicircle around their brother. The scale of the sitters is suggested by placing the two youngest below the level of the top of the table and by the huge mastiff beside the biggest child. The handling and colour throughout are of a quality unsurpassed in Van Dyck's English period; they are seen at their finest, perhaps, in the painting of the flesh and in the harmony of colours which set off the whites in the group composed by the two youngest children and their immediate background. The heads are painted with great sensitivity and the individual characters are enchantingly presented. The spectator is riveted by the slight cast in the eyes of the eldest child. It is particularly noticeable in the head of the Prince of Wales that the paint in a passage painted when the sitter was in front of him is more richly applied and carefully worked than in the surrounding areas which would have been worked up later. The same contrast in volume and texture can be seen particularly clearly in the double portrait of the Villiers boys (Millar, no.153) which Van Dyck had painted for the King two years earlier. The portrait of the Prince of Wales is very close to the single full-length in armour (Glück, 388) which was painted for the Earl of Newcastle and may have been based on the same sitting.

The composition was immediately popular and many copies and derivations are known; an early copy, on a small scale and matching the small copy of no.7, is at Woburn and may be by Van Leemput. The influence of the group can be seen in, for example, the decorations by Francis Cleyn in the North Drawing-Room at Ham House; in at least two mythological scenes by Lely; or in a group of the children of the 2nd Earl of Westmorland which was formerly at Apethorpe and which was an excellent example of the adaptation by a provincial painter of a design by Van Dyck to another purpose. The smaller dog appears, confusingly, in Cornelius Johnson's full-length of

Charles I, painted in 1631, at Chatsworth (Millar, no.152).

Her Majesty The Queen

27 Princess Elizabeth (1635–50) and Princess Anne (1637–40)

(COLOUR PLATE V, between pages 16 and 17)

Canvas, 29.8×41.9 ($11\frac{3}{4}$×$16\frac{1}{2}$)

Inscribed slightly later, and partly erroneously: *The Princesse/Elizabeth* and *Henry Duke of Glocester*. The younger Princess died so young (in 1640) that her existence may have been forgotten and the baby would have been identified therefore with the next royal child, who survived until 1660.

A sketch of the heads of the King's two youngest children as they were to appear in the large group painted in 1637 (no.26). The sketch would almost certainly have been painted in the house in which the children were in residence at the time. It establishes the touching relationship between them which Van Dyck developed on the final canvas, where the most obvious difference is in Princess Elizabeth's hair which escapes from her cap and falls across her forehead.

No.27 is the only surviving preparatory sketch of its kind from Van Dyck's English period. The heads are swiftly drawn on a silver-grey ground, with a suggestion of a darker area behind the elder child's head. The outline drawing in sienna is nervous and liquid; the forms are modelled in delicate pinks and greys.

The sketch was formerly in the possession of Lord Chesham (R.A., 1953–4, no.317; Agnew, 1968, no.49; *Age of Charles I*, no.106).

Private collection

28

28 Lady Henrietta Maria Stanley, later Countess of Strafford (1630–85)

Canvas, 76.8×61.9 (30¼×24⅜)

Inscribed: *Henriete Marie. Stanley./Æ^{ta} Suæ 7.*

Half-length, in a white dress, holding a bunch of roses on a stone ledge in front of her.

Daughter of the 7th Earl of Derby, who married the 2nd Earl of Strafford (no.32), as his first wife, in 1655. She was painted by Van Dyck with her parents in the group now in the Frick Collection (Glück, no.487); in no.28, which must have been painted in 1637–8 (she was born on 17 November 1630), she appears to be slightly older. A comparatively little-known, but enchanting, example of Van Dyck's sensitivity and understanding as a painter of children; it appears in the list, attached to her husband's will, of pictures which were to be preserved as heirlooms at Wentworth Woodhouse. A copy was sold at Sotheby's, 11 May 1960 (102); another is at Blair Castle (R.A., 1953–4, no.149).

Trustees of the Rt Hon Olive, Countess Fitzwilliam's Chattels Settlement. Lent by kind permission of Lady Juliet de Chair

29 Dorothy, Viscountess Andover (1611–91), and her sister Elizabeth, Lady Thimbleby

(COLOUR PLATE VI (DETAIL), between pages 16 and 17)

Canvas, 132.1×149.9 (52×59)

A double three-quarter-length group: the standing figure in silvery white with a warm grey or fawn scarf laced with gold, the seated figure in dull gold with a grey-brown scarf, receiving from Cupid, who wears a cool scarlet cloak, a basket of roses, two of which she holds in her right hand.

The sitters were the second and third daughters of Thomas, Viscount Savage. Dorothy married on 10 April 1637, against his father's wishes, Charles, Lord Andover, who in 1669 succeeded his father as Earl of Berkshire. Her younger sister, Elizabeth, had married on 29 September 1634 Sir John Thimbleby of Irnham in Lincolnshire. The hymeneal allusions in Cupid's offering roses to the seated sister probably relate to the later marriage.

The poised, almost frozen, positions taken up by the two main figures is only slightly disturbed by the rapid movement of Cupid into the group. The contrasts in colour are most carefully worked out and a high, clear key

73

brilliantly sustained. A particularly fine passage – the
contrast between Cupid's cool scarlet cloak and silver-
grey wings or between his golden hair and cool pinkish
golden flesh – foreshadows a passage in the later *Cupid and
Psyche* (no.58); but the rather evenly painted flesh and the
broad handling in, for instance, the whites, perhaps suggests a date near the time of Lady Andover's marriage.

The picture belonged to Lely and few pictures demon-
strate more clearly both the difference in spirit between
the two painters and the ages in which they flourished and
Lely's indebtedness to his predecessor. This lesson was
especially obvious when the picture, which was acquired
for £87 by the Earl of Sunderland, hung in the gallery at
Althorp surrounded by so many of Lely's female portraits,
a number of which Sunderland had commissioned. Evelyn, who saw the picture in Sunderland's lodgings in
Whitehall on 27 January 1685, described it as 'of incomparable performance'. In 1976 it was acquired by the
National Gallery in lieu of death duties. It is still in the
frame in which it hung at Althorp.

A copy is at Wardour Castle; others were formerly at
Hengrave and Kimbolton. The motive of Cupid offering
flowers was copied verbatim in a school piece of Lord and
Lady Bayning, Christie's, 16 November 1951 (18) (R.A.,
1953–4, no.130; Agnew, 1968, no.56; and information
kindly supplied by Mr Christopher Brown).

The Trustees of the National Gallery

30 Prince Charles Louis, Elector Palatine (1617–80), and Prince Rupert (1619–82)

Canvas, 132×152 (52×59⅞)

Inscribed: *CAROLVS PRENCEPS ELECTOR
PALATINVS/CVM FRATRE ROBERTO./1637*. The
inscription is of the type inscribed on a number of the
portraits by Van Dyck in Charles I's collection.

The two young men, the eldest surviving sons of the King and Queen of Bohemia, three-quarter-length in armour, the elder holding a baton and wearing the Lesser George on a chain round his neck; he had been made a Knight of the Garter in 1633.

Prince Charles Louis came to London in November 1635 to enlist his uncle's support in the recovery of his lands (his father had died in 1632); a cold and calculating youth, he also ingratiated himself with some of the leaders of the opposition to the King. Prince Rupert, who had been on active service under the Prince of Orange, joined his brother in February 1636. He was enchanted with life at the English court, became devoted to his uncle and to the Queen and was attracted into artistic and literary circles in London. He was described as 'of a rare condition, full of spirit and action . . . whatsoever he wills, he wills vehemently' (P. Morrah, *Prince Rupert of the Rhine* (1976), pp.35–46).

The double portrait, which must have been painted before the Princes departed from England on 26 June 1637, hung in the Privy Gallery at Whitehall in a frame 'adorned with Marshiall weapons carved whited and guilded' (*Van der Doort*, p.26). Sold in 1650 to Jasper Duart for £50, it was one of the pictures which Charles II's agents were particularly anxious to regain for him after the Restoration. It was, however, sold by Duart to Jabach and by him, in 1671, to Louis XIV (A. Roy, *Le XVIIᵉ siècle flamand au Louvre Histoire des collections* (Paris, 1977), pp.6–7, no.18; Musée du Louvre, *Catalogue sommaire illustré*, vol.1 (1979), p.52, Inv.1238).

Early copies are, for example, in the North Carolina Museum of Art and, on a small scale, at Warwick Castle. A variant of the portrait of the elder Prince, against a plain background, is recorded by Glück (514); the type was etched by Hollar (P.1447) in 1646; the head alone of Prince Charles Louis was one of the two portraits engraved after Van Dyck by John Payne (d. *c*.1640; Corbett and Norton, p.9); and the head of the younger Prince was engraved by Robert Peake. Van Dyck had painted the two Princes in The Hague very early in 1632 (see above, p.18); and during their stay in London he also painted single full-lengths of them (eg N.P.G. L124 and 125).

Musée du Louvre

31 Anne Crofts, Countess of Cleveland (d.1638)

(COLOUR PLATE VII, between pages 16 and 17)

Canvas, 104.8×82.9 (41¼×32⅝)

Inscribed, probably in an early eighteenth-century hand: *The Countess of Cleveland wife to/Tho.ˢ wentworth Earl of Cleveland:*

Half-length, to the front, holding roses on a ledge. Her blue dress is enriched with a brooch and jewelled clasps made in the form of *amorini*.

The sitter was the daughter of Sir John Crofts of Little Saxham. Her sister was the wife of Thomas Killigrew. She married, not long before 1612, Thomas, Lord Wentworth, Earl of Cleveland, and died on 1 January 1638.

The portrait is presumed to have passed, with the family group by Van Dyck (see no.73), in the female line (the Countess's only son died without male issue) to the 2nd Earl of Strafford, of the second creation (d.1791), and then to his nephew, George Byng. It was probably painted slightly earlier than the family group. At an early date it was set into the panelling of the hall at Wrotham Park, in a sequence of family portraits, and has apparently, until recently, escaped notice.

Private collection

32 The Children of the Earl of Strafford

Canvas, 208.3×163.8 (82×64½); the canvas has almost certainly been enlarged at the top at a later date.

A full-length group of the surviving children of Strafford by his second marriage, to Lady Arabella Holles, who had died in 1631: William (1626–95), who became Lord Raby in 1640, and his sisters, Lady Anne (1629–96), who married in 1654 the 2nd Lord Rockingham, and Lady Arabella (1630–89), who married Justin MacCarthy. William succeeded to his father's honours when the attainder was reversed in 1662. He was a supporter of William III at the Revolution. In no.32 the brother – 'a sweet-natured and handsome youth, full of noble parts, and of a rare understanding for his years' – stands in black beside his elder sister, in white; her arm is taken by the younger girl, who is in blue with a greyish scarf.

32

Presumably painted for Lord Strafford, who was deeply devoted to his children; it should, however, be noted that in Lely's sale, among his pictures by Van Dyck, was 'The Earl of *Strafford* and his two Sisters', measurements given as 185.4×160 (73×63) and sold for £81; and that no.32 does not appear in the list, attached to the will of the 2nd Earl of Strafford, of pictures which were to be preserved as heirlooms at Wentworth Woodhouse. The children's movements are elusive and it is not clear at what dates they would all have been in London. It has been suggested that the group was painted at the same time as no.23, when Wentworth had sent for his children to join him in London, but their ages, and perhaps their costumes, suggest a slightly later date. The rather heavy, loaded paint, which has affinities with no.62, may support such a suggestion. The head of the boy is very thick and creamy in texture. Lely, apart from apparently owning the picture, was probably influenced by it when he designed, in 1647, his group of the royal children in which the oldest child in the group is perhaps a reinterpretation of the figure of Lord Raby (*Sir Peter Lely*, N.P.G. (1978–9), no.7; R.A., 1953–4, no.230).

Trustees of the Rt Hon Olive, Countess Fitzwilliam's Chattels Settlement. Lent by kind permission of Lady Juliet de Chair

33 Anne Cavendish, Lady Rich (1612–38)

Canvas, 221.6×129.5 (87¼×51); the canvas was at a later date enlarged on all sides.

Inscribed: *Anne wife of Robert Lord/Rich Daughter of the Earle-/of Devonshire./about 1637. p. S.ᵣ Ant: Vandike.*

Full-length, standing, in a black dress with deep yellow linings to the sleeves and holding a rose across her waist. A pale scarlet curtain hangs down behind.

Daughter of the 3rd Earl of Devonshire, she married on 9 April 1632 Robert, Lord Rich, later 3rd Earl of Warwick. She died, on 24 August 1638, in her twenty-seventh year.

In the collection of the 4th Lord Wharton (see no.56). The portrait is finer in quality than a number of the family portraits in his collection, and was painted at a slightly earlier date. Even in so seemingly static a portrait, there is a good deal of restrained movement and a look of amusement in the sitter's face. It is instructive to compare it with the portrait of Lady Anne, probably by Cornelius Johnson, which was painted *c.*1628 and stitched on to the group (at Chatsworth) of her mother and her two brothers (C. H. Collins Baker, *Lely & the Stuart Portrait Painters* (1912), vol.I, p.58). The sitter's untimely death was lamented in verses by Sidney Godolphin and Waller. A central theme in Waller's poem was the friendship between Lady Rich and Lady Dorothy Sidney (no.40); 'the lovely passion each to other bare'.

It was among the Van Dycks sold in Lord Orford's sale, 1751, second day (54); subsequently in the Hardwick, De Grey and Lucas collections.

Private collection

33

34 Elizabeth Howard, Countess of Peterborough (1603–71)

Canvas, 231.1×125.1 (91×49¼); including at the top an addition of *c.*10.2 (4) and at the bottom of *c.*5.1 (2).

Inscribed: *Elizabeth Countess of Peterborough wife to/John Mordaunt Earl of Peterborough/Daughter & sole Heir to the L.ᵈ William/Howard son to charles Howard Earl of/Nottingham.*

Full-length, standing, in a white dress with blue bows, against an architectural background with a cool scarlet curtain on the left; she holds a pink rose over her dress.

The daughter of William, Lord Howard of Effingham, she had married before 7 April 1621 the 1st Earl of Peterborough. She was a lady of 'extraordinary beauty' and strong republican sympathies.

The portrait was established comparatively recently as the original of the design. Better-known copies are at Wilton, set into the panelling of the Double Cube Room and formerly identified as Lady Isabella Rich, and at Woburn (as Henrietta Maria). The canvas was fixed into the panelling of the King's Dining-Room at Drayton as

Elizabeth Countess of Peterborough wife to
John Mordaunt Earl of Peterborough
Daughter and sole heir to the Ld William
Howard son to charles Howard Earl of
Nottingham

34

part of a scheme of decoration carried out by Lady Peter-borough's eldest son, the 2nd Earl. It is probable that the inscription was put on, and the canvas enlarged, at that time.

The portrait is painted with great delicacy throughout – details of the head, cuffs and hands are especially brilliant – and the slight tilt of the head and movement of the dress, especially the folds lightly lifted by the Countess's left hand, convey most subtly a sense of movement. Such refinements are lacking in the copy at Wilton. Van Dyck's drawing for the upper part of the figure is in the British Museum (Vey, no.234v.; O. Millar, 'Van Dyck in London', *Burl. Mag.*, vol.CX (1968), pp.307–8; *Age of Charles I*, no 96).

L. G. Stopford Sackville, Esq

35 Anne Killigrew, Mrs Kirke (1607–41)

Canvas, 222.9×130.8 (87¾×51½); there is a later addition at the top of 7.6 (3).

Full-length, standing to the left front in a dress of deep gold with a grey scarf against a brownish curtain. She points with her right hand to a rose-bush which grows beside an elaborately carved urn. A small hound leaps up towards her.

The sitter was a sister of nos.38 and 39 and was a Dresser to the Queen. In 1627 she married George Kirke, Gentle-man of the King's Wardrobe, whose duties included pro-viding masquing apparel for the King and other perfor-mers. Mrs Kirke herself is recorded as a performer in masques. She was tragically drowned on 6 July 1641, when the Queen's barge capsized as it was being taken through London Bridge.

Probably painted *c*.1638, and an excellent instance of the richness of Van Dyck's colour and of his accomplished rendering of the accessories in his standard fashionable patterns. The portrait was in Lely's collection and was bought at his sale, 18 April 1682, by the Earl of Kent. It passed by descent through the De Grey, Cowper and Lucas collections, and was acquired by the Hon Clive Pearson in 1922. It was engraved in mezzotint by Isaac Beckett (R.A., 1953–4, no.129).

Parham Park, West Sussex

36 Mrs Endymion Porter (d.1663)

Canvas, 135.9×106.7 (53½×42)

Three-quarter-length, moving towards the left, in pastoral costume in a landscape and against a rocky background. She wears a deep red garment, flecked with gold, and holds a blue cloak that floats up behind her.

Daughter of Sir John Boteler, married in 1619 to Endym-ion Porter. She became one of the first converts to Cathol-icism among the ladies of Henrietta Maria's circle.

The sitter was formerly thought to be a member of the Devereux family. The Earl of Northumberland, however, is known to have possessed a portrait by Van Dyck of Mrs Porter, which Symonds saw at Northumberland House on 27 December 1652 and which appears in the Northumber-

35

land inventory of 1671, valued at £30, the sum affixed to the other female portraits, such as nos.40 and 41, on this scale. One of the portraits at Petworth (Collins Baker, *Petworth*, p.30, no.295), which in fact represents the Coun-tess of Dysart, has been mis-called Mrs Porter. In a set of slightly later standard copies of heads after Van Dyck, of the type usually attributed to 'Russell' or Van Leemput, sold in one of the Craven sales at Sotheby's, 27 November 1968 (26), was a copy of the head of no.36 bearing a contemporary inscription identifying the sitter as Mrs Porter.

The composition is one of the most dramatic among Van Dyck's female portraits, with a bold swinging move-ment which, with the informal, presumably Arcadian, attire, would have greatly impressed Lely. The modelling of the head is fresh, liquid and full and the eyes are particularly beautifully drawn. In mood the portrait is so different from those commissioned by Northumberland that it is possible that he acquired it, perhaps in the 1640s, when the Porters' lives and fortunes were in ruins and when Northumberland was certainly on the look-out for good pictures (Agnew, 1968, no.58).

The Duke of Northumberland

36

37

38

37 Sir Thomas Hanmer (1612–78)

Canvas, 110.5×88.3 (43½×34¾)

Half-length to the front in black, holding in his left hand the glove from his right hand which rests on his hip.

The sitter, who had succeeded to the baronetcy in 1624, was a page, and subsequently Cup-Bearer, at the court of Charles I. A man of civilized tastes, he made a copy of Norgate's *Miniatura* and his brother-in-law was Bernini's Mr Baker. He collected medals and became one of the most distinguished horticulturists of his time.

Probably painted *c*.1637. On 30 September 1638 Hanmer and his brother were granted a pass to travel for three years. John Evelyn, who knew him well and corresponded with him on gardening questions, saw the portrait on 14 January 1685 in the collection of Lord Newport among 'some excellent pictures, especialy that of Sir Tho: Hanmers of V: Dyke, one of the best he ever painted' (*Diary*, ed. E. S. de Beer, vol.IV, p.402). With no.39 it would have been among the 'several pictures of Vandyke' noted by Vertue in the Earl of Bradford's collection in 1714; it passed by descent to the present owner.

There is a spontaneous, lightly brushed and Venetian quality throughout the figure. Very fine passages include the drawing of the glove, the warm pinkish golden tone in the hand and the silvery tone in the glove. The form of the hand with the glove helps, with the poise of the figure, the gesture and the glance to suggest momentarily arrested movement. Before the discovery of the picture by the late Horace Buttery in 1958, and the realization that it was one of Van Dyck's most distinguished English portraits, the early references had been attached erroneously to the copy formerly in Cleveland (Glück, 438), but sold at Sotheby's, 7 December 1960 (48); other copies are recorded (O. Millar, 'Van Dyck and Sir Thomas Hanmer', *Burl. Mag.*, vol.C (1958), p.249; Agnew, no.54; *Age of Charles I*, no.103).

The Rt Hon The Earl of Bradford

38 Sir William Killigrew (1606–95)

Canvas, 104.1×82.6 (41×32½)

Inscribed, possibly in the hand of the artist: *SVR WILLIVM KILLIGREW/A. Van.Dyck.pinxit./1638.*

Half-length, to the right front, in black, resting his elbow on a ledge at the base of a column; a landscape in the background on the right.

The sitter was the eldest son of Sir Robert Killigrew and brother of nos.35 and 39; MP for Newport and Penryn in Cornwall, Governor of Pendennis Castle and Falmouth Haven and a Gentleman Usher to Charles I. In the Civil War he commanded one of the two troops of horse which guarded the King. After the Restoration he became Vice-Chamberlain to the Queen and was also a prolific dramatist.

The portrait is an archetypal example of the bridge that Van Dyck's portraits form between the Venetian painters he so much admired and the English painters of the eighteenth century who were so deeply influenced by him.

37 (detail)

The background can be compared with that in no.56 which is less rich in texture and colour. A drawing in the British Museum (Vey, no.292) may be a preliminary sketch for the portrait, but in it the sitter is in a more frontal position in relation to the spectator.

Formerly at Clumber, in the collection of the Earl of Lincoln, and sold at Christie's, 31 March 1939 (56); in the early nineteenth century in the possession of William Carpenter.

Private collection

39 Thomas Killigrew (1612–83)   *1638*

(COLOUR PLATE VIII, between pages 16 and 17)

Canvas, 106.1×86 (41¾×33⅞)

A contemporary inscription reads: *Ant van Dyck.F./.1638:*

Half-length to the front, wearing a breastplate and sash, resting his right hand on a mastiff, on whose collar are the remains of an inscription giving the owner's name (in the copy at Chatsworth this inscription can be clearly read,

combined with the Killigrew family crest).

The sitter was a dramatist and wit and an active royalist. He was a Page of Honour to Charles I and, during the Commonwealth, was Charles II's Resident in Venice. After the Restoration he was Groom of the Bedchamber and Master of the Revels and built and managed the Theatre Royal, Drury Lane. He was the brother of nos.38 and 35, and was married to Cecilia Crofts, sister of no.31. She died on 1 January 1638 and her sister died a fortnight later. These sad events are probably commemorated in the well-known portrait at Windsor of Thomas Killigrew with (?) his brother-in-law, also painted in 1638 (Millar, no.156).

The portrait, with the full-length of his sister Anne (no.35), was in the possession of Lely, who had probably secured them in the 1670s, when the Killigrews had fallen on hard times, or after the death in 1675 of Killigrew's brother-in-law George Kirke. It was (as *'il ritratto in mezza figura di Thomas Killigrew quando era giovane'*) one of the two pictures by Van Dyck which, from a number in the hands of Lely's heirs, the agent of the Grand Duke of Tuscany

81

40

recommended to his master. Lord Arlington also advised the Grand Duke to purchase them, '*per che erano l'opere megliori che tal huomo havesse fatto*', but his advice was ignored and the portrait was sold at Lely's sale for £83 to Lord Newport and has passed, with no.37, by descent to the present owner.

That no.39 is the original, rich in texture and exquisite alike in tone and touch, of a particularly beautiful portrait-pattern by Van Dyck is demonstrated by the alterations to the design which came to light when it was cleaned and restored in 1963. The area round the head, the drawing of the cuff on the left wrist, the fall of the right sleeve and the outline of the collar, appear to have been amended. More important, there are suggestions (scarlet under the breastplate and satin rather than steel on the left shoulder) that the breastplate may have been an afterthought by artist or patron. There is an important *pentimento* in the sitter's right hand; and the dog's head may originally have been set lower in the design and more completely in profile. The best-known copies are at Chatsworth (Glück, 396) and in the National Portrait Gallery (no.892; Piper, 1963, p.186; O. Millar, 'Van Dyck and Thomas Killigrew', *Burl. Mag.*, vol.cv (1963), p.385; Agnew, 1968, no.53).

The Rt Hon The Earl of Bradford

40 Lady Dorothy Sidney, Countess of Sunderland (1617–84)

Canvas, 136.2×109.2 (53⅝×43)

Three-quarter-length to the left, in a dark brown dress with deep orange-red sleeves and a pale brown-grey scarf, resting her left hand on the rim of a carved vase and pointing with her right to the blossoms that flower on the bush (? a rose) that is growing in it.

Daughter of the Earl of Leicester, whose wife was the sister of the 10th Earl of Northumberland. On 26 July 1639 she married the future 1st Earl of Sunderland, who was killed in 1643 at the battle of Newbury; in 1652 she married Robert Smythe. She was the 'Saccharissa' whom Edmund Waller celebrated in his poems.

One of the series of portraits of his female relations and friends which Northumberland commissioned from Van Dyck and which were still hanging in Northumberland House in 1671. As a series they can be seen, perhaps, in the European tradition of sets of portraits of beauties or famous ladies and they were the direct inspiration for Lely's female three-quarter-length portraits, different though they are in mood and atmosphere. Northumberland was, indeed, one of Lely's most important early patrons and the female portraits painted by Lely for Northumberland were clearly designed as further instalments in the sequence initiated by Van Dyck; Lely's portrait of Northumberland's daughter Elizabeth (fig.42), for example, is closely based on this particular Van Dyckian prototype. Four Countesses in Northumberland's original set (nos.40 and 41 and the Countesses of Devonshire and Carlisle) were engraved at an early date by Lombart, whose plates would have helped to disseminate the patterns. The frames on the Van Dycks at Pet-

Fig.42 Sir Peter Lely, *Lady Elizabeth Percy*. Petworth

worth (eg nos.23, 40 and 41) were made for the 6th Duke of Somerset by Parry Walton (G. Jackson-Stops in *Country Life*, 4 September 1980, pp.799–800, misreading his name as 'Perry Malton'). A copy in miniature in the manner of Hoskins is at Ham House (R.A., 1953–4, no.440).

The Lord Egremont, Petworth

41 Lady Anne Carr, Countess of Bedford (1615–84)

Canvas, 136.2×109.9 (53⅝×43¼)

Three-quarter-length in a blue dress with a grey-brown scarf, to the front, drawing a glove on to her right hand. Beside her is a rose-bush and behind a large carved vase.

Daughter of the former court favourite, the Earl of Somerset, and of the infamous Countess of Essex; she was born while her mother was a prisoner in the Tower. On 11 July 1637 she married William, Lord Russell, later 5th Earl of Bedford. When he returned from his travels no less than three of the young ladies who were to be painted by Van Dyck for Northumberland were mentioned as 'ripe for marriage; it is thought he will settle upon one of them'. Russell's father only agreed to marriage on the promise of a dowry of £12,000 from Somerset which he proved unable to pay. The marriage was happy and fruitful.

The most beautiful of the female portraits painted by Van Dyck for Northumberland (see no.40) and in every way one of Van Dyck's most magical portraits: the subtle sense of movement as the sitter moves imperceptibly forward is enhanced by the momentarily frozen movement in the hands, by the flutter of the scarf, 'A Lawne about the shoulders thrown', the stirring of the curtain and the

trembling of the rose-bush. The handling of the face and hair is exceedingly delicate and fresh, and the slight asymmetry in the sitter's eyes adds to the sense of a living sitter facing the painter. Van Dyck's preliminary pencil sketch is in the British Museum (Vey, no.241). A number of copies are recorded; there is nothing stylistically to warrant the attribution to Lely of a copy at Middachten. A copy is at Burghley; the copy at Woburn is probably by Symon Stone (R.A., 1953–4, no.442).

The Lord Egremont, Petworth

42 Portrait of a Girl as Erminia, attended by Cupid

Canvas, 109.2×129.5 (43×51)

Half-length, in a rocky landscape, standing to the left and looking over her shoulder at the spectator. She rests her left hand on a helmet and wears a breastplate over a red-gold garment with a green mantle on which Cupid stands, pointing to the right, out of the composition.

The design should probably not be linked with Bellori's record (p.261) of one of Van Dyck's English works: 'the portrait of a brown-haired Lady dressed as Pallas, armed, with a plume in her helmet and of a most beautiful and lively countenance' ('*una testa vaghissima, e viva*'). The girl is in the guise of Erminia, putting on the armour of her friend Clorinda, attended by Cupid, so that she may enter Jerusalem unrecognized and find the wounded Tancred (Tasso, *Gerusalemme Liberata*, bk.VI. 91–2). In Fairfax's translation the heroine is 'Stript to her petticote' under 'rugged steele'; there are references to her 'locks of shining

c 1638

gold' and 'tender arme'. Cupid is 'Fast by her side unseene'.

The helmet and the background are more freshly painted than the portrait; and the figure of Cupid has the clarity and freshness of touch of a comparable passage in Van Dyck's second Flemish period. The composition is inevitably rather uncomfortable, but the principal figure is a beautiful example of the elegant baroque movement and gestures which were to have so profound an effect on the design of portraits in England thereafter. Formerly in the Harford collection at Blaise Castle; with Agnew in 1913 (Glück, 408).

His Grace The Duke of Marlborough

43 Charles I and the Knights of the Garter in Procession

Panel, 29.2×131.8 ($11\frac{1}{2} \times 51\frac{7}{8}$); made up of two separate panels; on the back of each is the CR brand.

Painted for Charles I, probably in 1638, the sketch appears on the list of works, for which Van Dyck was asking the King for payment, as 'Le dessein, du Roy et tous les Chevaliers' (P.R.O., S.P. 16/406, 4; Hookham Carpenter, pp.67–8). It has always been associated with the passage in Bellori, pp.262–3, which describes a scheme, apparently submitted to the King by Sir Kenelm Digby, for a set of four tapestries, based on designs by Van Dyck, intended to be hung in a *'gran salone della Corte Regia'* at Whitehall and illustrating the history and ceremonial of the Garter. It has been suggested that the tapestries would have been used to deck the walls of the Banqueting House and were conceived as part of the decoration of the interior after Rubens's canvases had been set into the ceiling (see P. Palme, *Triumph of Peace* (1957), pp.282–8).

The *modello* is the only surviving visual evidence of the project and would presumably have been for, in Bellori's words, *'la Processione de' Cavalieri ne' loro habiti'* (Bellori indicates that the King at first baulked at the huge sum demanded by Van Dyck for his *'cartoni, e pitture'*, but that this would have been adjusted if the artist had not died; Van Dyck's scheme, however, may have presented other practical difficulties).

Formerly among the King's pictures which were in store or 'as yett unplaced', the sketch ('in black and white in oyle Cullors a long narrow peece – wch was made for a moddell for a – bigger peece where yor Ma^{ty} and the Lords of the Garters, goeing a Precessioning upon St Georgs day') was sold for £5 after the King's execution (*Van der Doort*, p.158; *Sale*, p.151) and subsequently belonged to Lely, who himself made a number of drawings of figures in a Garter procession (O. Millar in *Sir Peter Lely*, N.P.G

43

(1978–9), nos.86–116). Eventually acquired by Reynolds for the Duke of Rutland in the Earl of Northington's sale in 1787.

The only important precedent for the design was the etching by Marcus Gheeraerts the elder (1576) of the procession of the Knights of the Garter (A. M. Hind, *Engraving in England in the Sixteenth & Seventeenth Centuries*, vol.I (1952), pp.104–21). It is perhaps unlikely that Van Dyck had in mind any specific annual procession of the Garter Knights, but the procession in 1638 was particularly important as it preceded the installation of the Prince of Wales. Van Dyck's design is a fairly accurate picture of the grand procession to the Chapel (probably in Whitehall) on the Feast of St George's Day. A group of Gentlemen-at-Arms herald the approach of the King, whose train is borne by a cluster of noble youths and whose canopy is supported by four gentlemen. Before him walk a nobleman carrying the Sword of State; the officers of the Order; and twenty-five(?) Knights. The senior, probably the Earl of Mulgrave, walks alone nearest to the King; the two in front of him are probably the 4th Earl of Pembroke, the Lord Chamberlain (see no.12) and the Earl of Arundel, Earl Marshal (see no.21). Statues in the niches in the wall behind probably commemorate earlier Sovereigns of the Order; from the balcony above the procession is watched, it seems, by the Queen and her ladies. The King was deeply attached to the Order, removed its festival from Whitehall to Windsor and reorganized the services 'as patterns of the new High Church ceremonial so loathed by the Puritans' (R. Strong, *Charles I on Horseback* (1972), pp.59–63).

As a composition the sketch illustrates once more, on a small scale, Van Dyck's essentially two-dimensional sense of design and the flow of linear rhythms which had already been implicit in the *Continence of Scipio* (no.3) and had owed so much to Veronese, to whom a final debt is perhaps paid in the architectural backcloth which, like the background to, for example, *The Family of Darius before Alexander* in the National Gallery, runs unswervingly parallel to the surface of the picture. In handling and colour, as in composition, the style is now far from Rubens's technique in his oil sketches. The panel is painted in monochrome, heightened with white on a pale pinkish tone laid over a prepared white ground; there is no hint of local colour. The composition, especially of the figures, is set out almost entirely in line (much preliminary pencil drawing is still visible), though a line of an exceptional nervous beauty, very varied, sensitive and suggestive. The copious interplay, in the figures, of elegant gestures and complex movements, is characteristic of Van Dyck's double and group-portraits; but it is displayed along a very narrow and extended stage. Broad areas of thin pale brown paint, which has almost the consistency of watercolour, are used to define the architectural detail in the background (O. Millar, 'Charles I, Honthorst and Van Dyck', *Burl. Mag.* vol.xcvi (1954), pp.36–42; Vey, *Ölskizzen*, p.201; Agnew, 1968, no.60; *Age of Charles I*, no.85).

Trustees of Belvoir Estate

Narrow stage close & parallel to picture plane. Fluent & sinuous intertwining of frgs in which hands play important part.
Play of twists & twists in figures & groups — this very dif from V's predecessors. V - air of spontaneity

43 (detail)

44 Lord John Stuart (1621–44) with his brother, Lord Bernard Stuart, later Earl of Lichfield (1622–45)

(COLOUR PLATE IX, between pages 16 and 17)

Canvas, 237.5×146.1 (93½×57½); the original canvas has probably been enlarged on all sides.

Two full-length figures; the one standing on the left is in a golden doublet and dark brown breeches, the other, standing below him and turning to face the spectator, is in blue cloak and breeches, all laced with silver.

The younger sons of the 3rd Duke of Lennox, younger brothers of the Duke of Richmond (no.48) and of Lord George Stuart (no.59). Both fell on the royalist side in the Civil War. Lord John died of wounds received at the battle of Cheriton, 29 March 1644, when he was in command of the royalist horse: 'a young man of extraordinary hope . . . who, being of a more choleric and rough nature than other branches of that illustrious and princely family, was not delighted with the softness of the Court, but had dedicated himself to the profession of arms when he did not think the scene should have been in his own country. His courage was so signal that day that too much could not be expected from it if he had outlived it, and he was so generally beloved that he could not but be very generally lamented' (Clarendon, vol.III, p.338). The younger brother had been designated Earl of Lichfield before he fell at Rowton Heath, in command of the King's Troop, on 26 September 1645: 'a very faultless young man, of a most gentle, courteous, and affable nature, and of a spirit and courage invincible; whose loss . . . the King bore . . . with extraordinary grief' (ibid. vol.IV, pp.115–16).

Early in 1639 the brothers had set off on a three-year tour of the Continent, and they must have sat to Van Dyck just before their departure. No.76 is Van Dyck's preparatory study for the pose of the younger brother. The composition is one of the most brilliant produced by Van Dyck during his years at the English court. The elegant pose struck by each, the rich contrast in colour, the flowing rhythms which link the two figures and the dramatic setting of the younger boy's figure with his glance across his shoulder towards the spectator – a possible reminiscence of Correggio – epitomize the revolution which Van Dyck brought about in English painting. These qualities are also displayed in the double portrait at Althorp (the *Pembroke Family* (fig.31), and in microcosm in the sketch for the *Garter Procession* (no.43).

The picture passed to the sister of the last Duke of Richmond and Lennox (who died in 1672) and ultimately to her granddaughter, the 1st Countess of Darnley; subsequently in the possession of the Earls of Darnley, Sir George Donaldson, Sir Ernest Cassel and the Countess Mountbatten of Burma.

In the eighteenth century, when it hung at Cobham Hall, it so impressed Gainsborough (who painted the 4th Earl of Darnley in 1785) that he was moved to paint the copy now in St Louis Art Museum (R. R. Wark, 'A Note on Gainsborough and Van Dyck', *Museum Monographs III*, St Louis Art Museum (1974), pp.45–53). It may also have inspired the double portrait of two unidentified young

45

men, painted in the style of Van Dyck, in the National Gallery (no.3605; Martin, *Catalogue*, pp.63–7) (R.A., 1953–4, no.139).

The Broadlands Collection

45 William Howard, later Viscount Stafford (1612–80)

Canvas, 106.7×83.8 (42×33); there is apparently a later addition to the canvas at the top.

Half-length in black, against a plain background, wearing the ribbon of the Bath.

The second surviving son of the Earl of Arundel, brought up in the Roman Catholic faith. He wrote an important biographical notice of his father and something of his enthusiasm for works of art. Quarrelsome, unpopular and a staunch Catholic, he was beheaded on 29 December 1680 for complicity in the Popish Plot. He was 'not a man beloved, especially of his own family' and had been 'guilty of great vices in his youth'.

Probably painted *c*.1638. A drawing in the British Museum (Vey, no.221) is probably a preliminary sketch for this portrait. The sitter had accompanied his father on the Embassy to Germany in 1636 and in July 1639 he went to Holland with the Elector Palatine (see no.30). The portrait passed to the sitter's descendant, the Earl of Stafford, and was seen at Tart Hall by Vertue: 'with a red ribband about ½ len in black painted by Vandyke'. It was apparently sold in 1743 (Vertue, vol.IV, p.166, vol.V,

46

47

pp.26 and 59) and was acquired subsequently by the 1st Marquess of Bute. It was at Luton Park by 1799. The pattern is close to that of no.47. A copy is at Arundel (Glück, note to 513; information from Miss Catherine Armet).

Private collection

46 **Portrait of an unknown Man**

Canvas, 133×95 (52⅜×37⅜)

Three-quarter-length in black, looking to the left and leaning his right arm on a ledge.

Recently attributed to Tiberio Tinelli; but the traditional attribution was to Van Dyck and it is an excellent and weighty example of his English style, with a particularly warmly and sensitively painted head and a rich, nervous touch in the whites (there are *pentimenti* in the collar).

The provenance of the portrait is not known; it was first mentioned in the Uffizi inventory of 1704 (no.1850), when it was hanging in the Tribuna (M. Webster in *Firenze e l'Inghilterra Rapporti artistici e culturali dal XVI al XX Secolo*, Palazzo Pitti (1971), no.32).

Galleria Palatina, Palazzo Pitti, Florence

47 **Sir Walter Pye** (1610–59)

Canvas, 106×85.7 (41¾×33¾)

Half-length to the front in black, holding his cloak across his body with his right hand.

Hitherto one of the portraits at Arundel in which the sitter has been loosely described as 'Lord Maltravers' (eg by Larsen, no.762; his no.763 *is* Lord Maltravers, but his no.764, again, is not). It has recently been identified by Malcolm Rogers as the portrait of Sir William Pye which was in Lely's collection and was bought at his sale for £40 by Lord Newport (see also no.39). The portrait appeared at Christie's, as a portrait of Arundel, in 1818, and by about 1850 it had entered the Duke of Norfolk's collection.

Sir Walter Pye of Mynde Park, near Kilpeck, who had been knighted in 1630, was MP for Herefordshire and for Wendover in the Short Parliament. He was at Oxford when the city surrendered to the Parliament in 1646. He probably sat to Van Dyck *c*.1638. The portrait is a good, strongly painted, example of a standard pattern (see no.45 for a variant upon it) which, as Malcolm Rogers has pointed out, was used by Van Dyck's imitators and, significantly, by Lely, notably in one of his portraits of the Duke of Lauderdale. The whites at the wrist are particularly fine. There are apparently *pentimenti* in the outlines of the figure; and it is not clear whether the background, which may have been intended to be a conventional glimpse of sky, framed by a ledge and a column, was ever finished (M. Rogers, 'Two Portraits by Van Dyck Identified', *Burl. Mag.*, vol.CXXIV (1982), pp.235–6).

His Grace the Duke of Norfolk, CB, CBE, MC, DL

48 James Stuart, 4th Duke of Lennox and 1st Duke of Richmond (1612–55)

Canvas, 99.7×160 (39¼×63)
Inscribed: *L·Steward/Duke of Richmond.*

Half-length, seated, in informal dress, a white shirt with a length of scarlet over his right shoulder. His right hand rests on the shoulder of a large hound and a boar-spear is propped up behind him.

The eldest brother of nos.44 and 61, he succeeded to the Dukedom of Lennox in 1624 and was created Duke of Richmond on 8 August 1641. On 5 December 1641 he was appointed Lord Steward. He filled many offices of state and was a devoted supporter of the King. Before the Civil War he lent him £30,000 and during the war he advanced a further £66,000: 'a most excellent, loyall, prudent, and religious person; one who had attended his Majestie throughout all this warr' (Warwick, p.302). He was very dear to the King and was entrusted with his burial in St George's Chapel.

The Duke sat at least twice to Van Dyck: once for a frontal portrait, and on another ocasion for a head turned to the left which was used by Van Dyck in a portrait, as Paris (of which the best known version is in the Louvre), and also in the full-length in the Metropolitan Museum (Glück, 410 and 411). The quality of the former is unexpectedly disappointing; and, although the portrait in New York is a magnificent piece, the head is rather dull – certainly less sensitive and deeply-felt than the head in no.48, in which the sitter is probably slightly older and for

which a fresh sitting may have been necessary. The hound, which is also prominent in the portrait in New York, is stated to have saved his master's life, possibly in a boar-hunt, to which the weapon would be an obvious allusion, and which may have taken place during the Duke's travels on the Continent, 1630–3.

The portrait, which was acquired by the Earl of Iveagh in 1889, had been formerly at Penshurst. It appears on a list, dated 2 September 1659, of pictures given by the Countess of Leicester, sister of no.24, to her son, Henry Sidney: 'Duke of Richmond wth a Greyhound, A halfe figure. Originall by Vandyke'. An early copy is in the Laughton collection in Scarborough (MS at Penshurst, vol.VII; P. Murray in *Catalogue of the Paintings*, Iveagh Bequest, 2nd edn. (1960), pp.12–13, no.48).

The Iveagh Bequest, Kenwood (GLC)

c 1639

49

50

49 Sir John Borlase (1619–72)

Canvas, 137×107.5 ($53\frac{13}{16}$×$42\frac{5}{16}$)

Three-quarter-length to the front, in black, against a plain dark background, leaning his right arm upon a ledge.

The sitter, MP for Great Marlow, 1640, Corfe Castle, 1641, and, after the Restoration, High Wycombe, was a staunch royalist who was created a baronet in 1642 and was, at a later date, imprisoned. He married on 4 December 1637 the daughter (no.50) of Sir John Bankes. The portraits were probably painted soon after the marriage. They are still in the fine frames which, after the Restoration, Lady Borlase's brother, Sir Ralph Bankes, commissioned for them and for later family portraits by, for example, Sir Peter Lely (R.A., 1953–4, no.229).

The National Trust, Kingston Lacy

50 Lady Borlase (d.1683)

Canvas, 137×107.5 ($53\frac{13}{16}$×$42\frac{5}{16}$)

Three-quarter-length, standing to the left against a plain background, in a white dress with a blue scarf held across her body with her right hand. A vase of roses stands beside her on a ledge.

Alice, eldest daughter of Sir John Bankes, Lord Chief Justice of the Common Pleas, and of the Lady Bankes who defended Corfe Castle in the Civil War. The position of her right hand and the proximity of the vase of roses may suggest that she was with child when she sat to Van Dyck. She was converted to Roman Catholicism in her widow-

hood and died in Paris (R.A., 1953–4, no.231).

The two portraits are freshly painted (especially in and round the heads) with evidence of alteration in course of painting in, for example, the shape of the slash on the husband's sleeve and in the line of Lady Borlase's dress across her bosom. The treatment of such passages as her dress and scarf has, by this late date, become fairly simple. The pattern of the male portrait – black and white against plain warm dark brown – is suggestive of some of Lely's earliest portraits.

The National Trust, Kingston Lacy

51 Margaret Smith, Mrs Thomas Carey and later Lady Herbert

Canvas, 218.4×137.2 (86×54)

Inscribed: *Margarett smith wife of Thomas/Carye of ye bed Chamber 2^d brother/of Philadelphia Mother of Philip/now Lord Wharton,/about 1636,/p.s.^{r} Ant: Vandike.*

Full-length, moving to the right on a high step and against a dark background, in a blue-green dress with a light grey-brown scarf.

Daughter of Sir Thomas Smith, Master of the Requests, she married first Thomas Carey, son of the 1st Earl of Monmouth and a Gentleman of the Bedchamber. He died on 9 April 1634, and she married secondly Sir Edward Herbert, Attorney-General to the Queen and subsequently Lord Keeper.

Thomas Carey's sister, Philadelphia, was the mother of Lord Wharton, for whose gallery of Van Dycks no.51 was

51

52

painted. The two portraits (nos.51 and 52) from the collection of the late Lord Wharton have featured little in the literature on Van Dyck. They were not included in the sale to Catherine the Great. No.51 passed to Horace Walpole and was in the sale at Strawberry Hill, 25 April 1842 *et seq.*, twentieth day (87). Later in the possession of Lord Wharton, sold at Sotheby's, 17 November 1948 (19), bought in.

No.51 has much of the charm and movement which Van Dyck introduced into the English portrait and such details as the whites, the jewels, and the painting of the dress and the hair seem wholly autograph. The odd staging of the figures in both portraits may be connected with the places they occupied, or were painted to fill, in the original room in which Wharton hung his pictures.

Major Malcolm Munthe, MC

52 Jane Goodwin, Lady Wharton (1618–58)

Canvas, 218.4×137.2 (86×54)

Inscribed: *Iane sole Daughter and heyre/of Arthur Goodwin 2ᵈ Wife of/Philip now Lord Wharton,/1639 about yᵉ age of 21/p. sʳ Ant: Vandike.*

Full-length, standing on a rocky ledge, in a white dress, picking roses from a bush that grows in a carved vase on the left.

Daughter and heiress of Arthur Goodwin (no.55), she married Lord Wharton as his second wife on 7 September 1637. The portrait was in Lord Wharton's collection (see no.51), but was sold in Lord Orford's sale, 1751, second day (53). Eventually in the collection of the late Lord Wharton, sold at Sotheby's, 17 November 1948 (20), bought in. There are passages in which Van Dyck's method in building up a picture can be discerned. The sky, for instance, is brushed roughly round the very freely painted foliage; and the greyish background is worked up to the head, leaving gaps at the back of the head. The handling throughout is fresh and swift.

Major Malcolm Munthe, MC

93

53 Queen Henrietta Maria (1609–69)

(COLOUR PLATE X, between pages 16 and 17)

Canvas, 71.8×56.5 (28¼×22¼)

Head and shoulders, in profile to the left, in a white dress with a light brown scarf.

Bernini's bust of the King, carved on the basis of the study of the King's countenance specially painted by Van Dyck (no.22), had been so successful that the Queen wished to commission from Bernini a companion bust of herself. She wrote to him, therefore, in June 1639 and informed him that the necessary portraits would be provided for Bernini's use by George Con, the Papal Agent to the Queen in London. It is clear, however, that as early as August 1637 the Papal court had been informed of the Queen's wishes; and in November 1637 Cardinal Barberini had been told that she had at last allowed herself to be painted in the three positions which the sculptor would need. She continued, however, to procrastinate and not until late in June 1638 was Con able to report that the King had agreed to let the Queen have an undisturbed week while he went hunting, so that she could be painted. Con was to meet Van Dyck in Greenwich, where the Queen was in residence, to see if it was feasible to make a single portrait for Bernini's use. This proved impossible; but on 27 August 1638 Con reported that the Queen had at last put on display the portraits painted for the making of the bust and that they would be dispatched on the first good occasion (I am deeply indebted to Mr Ronald Lightbown for his characteristic generosity in making available to me his transcripts from the Vatican Library, Barb. Lat. 8645, on which this account is based).

The portraits were never dispatched. Baldinucci gave as the reason for this the civil disorders – 'le turbolenze' – which were soon to break out in England; but it should also be remembered that Bernini had told Nicholas Stone, when he met him on 22 October 1638, that he had refused to execute another bust on the basis of a painting, even 'if thaire were best picture done by the hand of Raphyell'.

Although three portraits had been produced for Bernini (the frontal head is at Windsor: Millar, no.148), only two portraits of the Queen, 'pour Mons Barnino', appear (at £15) on the 'Memoire' of works, painted for the Crown, for which Van Dyck was requesting payment. The third canvas (see no.54) may already have been given away or in some way detached from the set.

As he had done in no.22, Van Dyck exerted himself at this comparatively late date to produce, in a style as delicate and sensitive as at any point in his career, an image of the utmost refinement. The scarf is floated over the fully modelled white sleeve. The pale blue bows are lightly painted over the underpaint and their forms are defined characteristically by shadows applied afterwards and in slightly thicker paint. The form, and individual passages of detail, of the lace collar are brilliantly expressed.

Originally Van Dyck had painted in no.53 the Queen's right hand, lightly holding the scarf away from her bosom. At some date between 1763 and 1787 this was painted out, but it can clearly be seen in X-ray (and can even be discerned with the naked eye) and the position of the scarf

54

·is meaningless without it. The original design can be seen in early copies (eg at Merton College, Oxford). In an odd derivation in the Pitti (Inv. Palatina, no.331) the design is extended almost to a half-length and the Queen holds a rose in her left hand; the right hand is omitted (*Firenze e l'Inghilterra Rapporti artistici e culturali dal XVI al XX Secolo*, Palazzo Pitti (1971), no.18; Millar, no.149).

Her Majesty The Queen

54 Queen Henrietta Maria (1609–69)

Canvas, 63.5×52.1 (25×20½)

Head and shoulders, in profile to the right.

See no.53. The portrait appears to have been separated from its companions at a very early date, almost as soon as it had become clear that Bernini was not going to undertake the marble bust of the Queen. The King or Queen probably gave the picture to the Duke of Hamilton (no.60), in whose inventories it appears: 'One peice of the queene to the waste syde faced of Sʳ Anthonye Vandyke'. It remained in the Hamilton collection until the Hamilton Palace sale, Christie's, 17 June 1882 (75); subsequently in the possession of J. E. Reiss, G. L. Bevan, Mrs Bevan and Warner S. McCall, from whom it was purchased for the Brooks Memorial Art Gallery in 1943. An accurate provenance for the portrait has been established by Martha J. Nolen of the Brooks Art Gallery (in a pamphlet issued by the Gallery). The early copy, which was for-

55

56

merly in the collection of the Earl of Denbigh, is in the National Maritime Museum; a good copy is at Nostell Priory; a copy in miniature, attributed to Des Granges, is at Windsor.

Brooks Memorial Art Gallery, Memphis, Tennessee (43.30/Warner S. McCall Collection)

55 Arthur Goodwin (1593/4–1643)

Canvas, 218.4×130.8 (86×51½)

Inscribed: *p. S.ʳ Ant: Vandike. Arthur Goodwin father of Iane/his sole daughter and heyre/2ᵈ wife of Philip now Lᵈ Wharton/1639 about yᵉ age of 40,*

Full-length, standing, in brown-grey breeches and a golden-brown doublet, holding his cloak, which is brown with a golden lining, across his chest; a pale red curtain hangs down behind.

A rich and influential Buckinghamshire landowner and a close friend of John Hampden, with whom he was at Magdalen, Oxford, where they composed Latin poems on the death of Henry, Prince of Wales. MP, 1620–6, for

Chipping Wycombe and Aylesbury and, in 1640, returned for the county with Hampden. In the Civil War he commanded a regiment of Buckinghamshire cavalry and he was appointed in 1643 to command the Parliament's forces in the county; he was at Hampden's side when he died of wounds received at Chalgrove Field.

The portrait was painted for Lord Wharton, who had married his daughter and heiress (no.52). It was eventually given by Sir Robert Walpole to the 3rd Duke of Devonshire. It is, in colour, one of Van Dyck's most harmonious portraits and the head is freshly and incisively modelled although it is, perhaps, a little at odds with the slightly dandified stance (R.A., *British Portraits*, 1956–7, no.72; *Age of Charles I*, no.94).

The Trustees of the Chatsworth Settlement

56 Philadelphia and Elizabeth Wharton

Canvas, 162×130 (63¾×51 3/16)

Inscribed: *Philadelphia Wharton and Elizabeth/Wharton yᵉ onely daughters of Philip/now Lord Wharton by Elizabeth his/first wife. 1640 about yᵉ age of 4 & 5. p. Sʳ Ant: Vandike.*

Full-lengths, standing, with a spaniel, against a pale green curtain with a landscape in the left background. The elder child is in white with a pale grey-brown scarf; the younger is in bright blue.

The children were daughters of Philip, 4th Lord Wharton, by his first wife, Elizabeth, daughter of Sir Rowland Wandesford; Elizabeth Wharton married, as his second wife, the 3rd Earl of Lindsey and died in 1669. Lord Wharton assembled, by acquisition as well as commission, a very large collection of portraits by Van Dyck, chiefly of his relations, but also of contemporaries such as Archbishop Laud, the Countesses of Chesterfield and Carlisle, the Marchioness of Worcester and Lady Rich (no.33). The King and Queen commissioned full-lengths from Van Dyck to be given to him. In the time of his son, the Marquess of Wharton, the portraits made a great impression in Lord Wharton's gallery at Upper Winchendon: Houbraken noted thirty-two portraits, including fourteen full-lengths (*De Groote Schouburgh*, vol.I (Amsterdam, 1718), edn. of 1943, p.147, and Vertue, vol.I, pp.29, 109; vol.III, pp.11–12).

The Marquess's successor, the Duke of Wharton, however, dispersed the collection. The greater number of the portraits by Van Dyck were acquired in 1725 by Sir Robert Walpole and of these the majority, in turn, went to St Petersburg when the Houghton pictures were bought by Catherine the Great in 1779.

At an early date, but not within the lifetime of Van Dyck, a standard form of inscription was put on Wharton's pictures. The dating cannot always be accepted without reserve, but the family portraits had probably been, in the main, produced towards the end of Van Dyck's life; it is perhaps unwise, on the other hand, to question the identities, over which Lord Wharton is unlikely to have been mistaken, as was done in the recent catalogue (see below) of the Van Dycks in The Hermitage. The two heads in no.56 are among Van Dyck's most touching child portraits, and are most delicately painted; but the prevailing tone is cold and there are passages of harsh drawing elsewhere throughout the design – even in the hands – and the landscape in particular is so cold, and so poorly drawn, that it must have been the work of an assistant. There are *pentimenti* in the outline of the dresses against the foreground (Varvshavskaya, pp.124–5, no.19).

The Hermitage, Leningrad

Fig.43 *Thomas Wentworth, 1st Earl of Strafford.* The Duke of Grafton

Fig.44 Titian, *Georges d'Armagnac with Guillaume Philandrier.* The Duke of Northumberland

Fig.45 John Shackleton, *Henry Pelham with John Roberts.* Private collection

57 Thomas Wentworth, 1st Earl of Strafford (1593–1641), with Sir Philip Mainwaring (1589–1661)

(COLOUR PLATE XI, between pages 16 and 17)

Canvas, 123.2×139.7 (48½×55)

Seated to the front in black, a sheet of paper in his hand, dictating to his Secretary, in red, who is seated at his elbow; a deep red-gold curtain hangs down behind.

Presumably painted between the return of Wentworth to London in September 1639 and the King's bestowal on him of the Garter on 12 September 1640. Philip Mainwaring, a Cheshire gentleman, son of Sir Randle Mainwaring of Over Peover, had been Wentworth's Secretary of State since his appointment as Lord Deputy. Justly famous though it is as a composition, and as a psychological study of the relationship between a great man and his secretary, the head of the principal figure is not of outstanding quality, although it illustrates vividly the remembrance by Sir Philip Warwick (p.112): 'His countenance was cloudy, whilst he moved, or sat thinking'. The head is apparently derived from the slightly earlier portrait of Wentworth in armour of which the probable original is at Euston (fig.43) and in which Van Dyck was again, or so he thought, paying tribute to Titian.

More important: the composition is a reinterpretation of Titian's portrait (fig.44) of Georges d'Armagnac with his secretary, Guillaume Philandrier (Wethey, vol.II, no.8). This was a popular and much-copied composition, of which the original was, in Van Dyck's time, in Northumberland's collection (it is now at Alnwick). Van Dyck was, in other words, consciously adapting, in Wentworth's service, a picture which belonged to one of the sitter's closest friends and one of Van Dyck's steadiest patrons. Van Dyck and Wentworth would also have known Sebastiano del Piombo's portrait of Cardinal Carondolet and his secretaries (Thyssen-Bornemisza Collection) which influenced Titian's pattern and, in Van Dyck's time, was at Arundel House. The original Titian had earlier been in the collection of the Duke of Buckingham, where Van Dyck may first have seen it.

Van Dyck's composition was much copied[1] and, as one of his most remarkable English works, had an influence which illustrates in microcosm his importance in the British school. Iconographically the theme is repeated in, for instance, Kneller's portrait of Prince George of Denmark with George Clarke at All Souls; but the composition was virtually copied by Shackleton, for instance, for Henry Pelham in the portrait (fig.45) with his secretary, John Roberts; and a reinterpretation was designed by Reynolds in his portrait, now in the Fitzwilliam Museum, of Rockingham (who owned the original Van Dyck) with Edmund Burke (see M. Jaffé, 'The Picture of the Secretary of Titian', *Burl. Mag.*, vol.CVIII (1966), pp.114–26).

Trustees of the Rt Hon Olive, Countess Fitzwilliam's Chattels Settlement. Lent by kind permission of Lady Juliet de Chair

[1]A large number of copies are recorded. In a copy in a private collection in Scotland the inscription on the paper held by Wentworth is almost legible.

58

c1640

58 Cupid and Psyche

Canvas, 199.4×191.8 (78½×75½); there are early additions at the top, between 9.5 and 10.8 (3¾ and 4¼), and bottom, c.5.7 (2¼). In Charles I's inventory the measurements are given as 188×195.6 (74×77).

The moment in the story of Cupid and Psyche, as told by Apuleius (*The Golden Ass*, ch.III), when Cupid discovers Psyche in the 'dull lethargy' of sleep into which she had sunk after she had yielded to the temptation to open the 'box of beauty' which Venus had asked her to bring back from Proserpine.

Painted for the King and recorded, as an insertion in Van der Doort's hand (p.43), in the King's Gallery at Whitehall, unframed. It is the only mythological picture known to survive from Van Dyck's English years. It was clearly painted towards the end of his life, but its original purpose is not clear. A masque by Shakerley Marmion (1637), based on the story of Cupid and Psyche, was performed while Prince Charles Louis was in England (see no.30). The story provided the subjects for the series of canvases (none of which survives) which were painted for the Queen's Cabinet at Greenwich by Rubens and Jordaens. This scheme was probably initiated in October 1639. The episode which Van Dyck painted was to figure also in a canvas by Jordaens of about the same proportions. Jordaens's style may not have pleased the Queen; and if one considers his work of the period (see, for example, R.-A. d'Hulst, *Jacob Jordaens* (1982), pls.144–7 or 154–6) and remembers the King's wish that in pictures for the room the faces of the women were to be as beautiful as possible and 'yᵉ figures gracious and svelta', one could imagine that a contribution by Van Dyck would have been more pleasing. '*Une piece pour la Maison a Grunwitz*', at £100, was among the pictures for which Van Dyck was, in his 'Memoire', asking to be paid by the Crown.

The composition, the latest of its kind to survive in Van Dyck's *œuvre*, marks the ultimate stage in his development from the days when he had been deeply under the influence of Rubens to a point where he had shed all that he absorbed in Flanders, retained his devotion to Titian and Veronese and had evolved a proto-rococo style which foreshadows the work, particularly, of French decorative painters at the turn of the century. The large mythological canvases of his second Flemish period have remarkable points of contact with such painters as La Fosse, Coypel or Boucher; and on a smaller scale his late mythologies begin, particularly in colour, to suggest links with Watteau.

In no.58 there is the same easy, supple movement, combined with a sense of poise or tension, which characterizes so many of Van Dyck's English portraits. The range of colours in the foreground is in a high key. Psyche's pinkish flesh contrasts with the cooler or more bronzed flesh of Cupid, although his face is warmer; he is crowned with golden curls and sprouts silvery wings. His pale scarlet cloak and fluttering blue ribbons are set against the clear blue cloak and white drapery on which Psyche reclines. Psyche's face, which was perhaps modelled on the painter's mistress (see no.80), is lightly and sensitively drawn; and the figures are handled throughout with considerable freshness. A particularly fine passage is the hand of Cupid which clasps his bow, painted in a characteristic pinkish indian red tone. The background is painted up to the figures, up to, for example, the basic shape of Cupid's wings which are then enlivened with fresh silvery impasto to soften the underlying outlines.

Copies are recorded; and Symon Stone was paid for a copy, painted for the Earl of Bath, in 1661. The design was engraved, in mezzotint, on a reduced format, by Bernard Lens (Millar, no.166).

Her Majesty The Queen

59 Thomas Howard, 2nd Earl of Arundel (1585–1646), with Aletheia, Countess of Arundel (d.1654)

Canvas, 139.7×212.7 (55×83¾)

Three-quarter-lengths, seated, wearing parliament robes. The Earl wears armour under his robe and holds the Earl Marshal's baton prominently in his left hand. He points to the island of Madagascar on a large globe; and the Countess, who holds an astrolabe in her lap, points with a pair of dividers to the same spot on the globe. A sheet, with drawings of the family's heraldic animals and bearing Arundel's motto (*CONCORDIA CVM CANDORE*), rests against the globe. On the right are papers, books and two classical busts.

The Earl had married in 1605 Aletheia Talbot, daughter and eventually sole heiress of the Earl of Shrewsbury and granddaughter of the Countess Dowager, 'Bess of Hardwick'. She brought him a fortune and shared his love of travel and works of art.

The composition records the revival in the second half of 1639 of the 'Madagascar Scheme': the colonization of the island by the Earl, with the King's approval. Ships were prepared and victualled and volunteers were recruited, but, perhaps because of Arundel's illness, the project was abandoned. The best-known version is in Vienna (Glück, 472); but it is, although a good contemporary version, not so fresh in quality as the version at

Arundel which is presumably the one which belonged to the Earl. In a copy at Knole the figure of the Earl's librarian, Francis Junius, is introduced in the background; another copy is at Swynnerton. A version appears hanging in the picture of a gallery, by Gonzales Coques, in The Mauritshuis (no.238); the principal figures are adapted by Fruytiers in his watercolour family group of 1643. There is a copy of the head of the Countess alone at Arundel; and the head of the Countess was etched by Hollar in Antwerp in 1646 (P.1354). The original composition was engraved by Vorsterman (Hervey, pp.418–19, 478).

His Grace the Duke of Norfolk, CB, CBE, MC, DL

60 James Hamilton, 3rd Marquess, and later 1st Duke, of Hamilton (1606–49)

Canvas, 218.4×129.5 (86×51)

Full-length, in armour, standing in a landscape, holding a baton in his right hand and resting his left on his helmet. He wears the badge of the Garter on a chain.

The sitter was one of the King's most trusted servants and exercised even more influence in Scotland than Lennox. He had borne the Sword at the King's Coronation and was a Gentleman of the Bedchamber and, 1628–44, Master of the Horse. In 1631 he had commanded the troops sent to assist the King of Sweden. In June 1639 he

Fig.46 David Scougall, *William Kerr, 3rd Earl of Lothian*. The Marquess of Lothian

60

was in command against the Covenanters. Defeated by Cromwell at Preston in 1648, leading a Scottish force which had invaded England in the royalist cause, he was beheaded a few weeks after the King. 'The aire of his countenance had such a cloud on it, that nature seems to have imprest *aliquid insigne*' (Warwick, p.103).

The Marquess played an active part in the growth of the King's collections. He brought important Northern pictures back for the King from his campaign, he exchanged pictures with him and even won a Mantua picture off the King in a wager. He himself owned a very fine collection, partly inherited from his father and partly acquired in Venice by his brother-in-law, Lord Feilding. A number of portraits by Van Dyck are listed in the inventories (in the Duke of Hamilton's possession) of his collection. 'My Lo: picture of Vandike' is recorded in an inventory of *c*. 1643 as are a number of portraits after Van Dyck. In another inventory no.60 appears as: 'One peice of my lords at length in armor of Sᵣ Anthony:Vandyke'. It is a good example of Van Dyck's very late English style; a copy in the Scottish National Portrait Gallery bears a

near-contemporary inscription with the date 1640. The tonality – steely silvers and blues against varied browns and fawns – is characteristic of Van Dyck's last phase; so, perhaps, are the pallid background and rather cold flesh tones and a passage such as the shorthand treatment of the foliage lower left: painted very thinly and then swiftly outlined and articulated in opaque reddish brown. The background is treated in the same summary fashion, perhaps because Van Dyck had used it earlier in his full-length of Lady Clanbrassil (fig.26). There is evidence to the naked eye of a slight change in the outline of the far leg and thigh; and the change of tone round the head, which is sensitively modelled, indicates clearly the area worked on by Van Dyck when he was actually engaged on the portrait.

A number of copies and derivations are recorded and the pattern was used – but not by Van Dyck – for other sitters. A particularly interesting derivation is the portrait of the 3rd Earl of Lothian (fig.46), in the Marquess of Lothian's collection, in which the setting is taken over complete by David Scougall. The posture is also used in a three-quarter-length of the Earl of Craven (see Sara Stevenson, 'Armour in Seventeenth-Century Portraits', *Scottish Weapons and Fortifications 1100–1800*, ed. D. H. Caldwell (1981), pp.339–77).

The Duke of Hamilton

61

Fig.48 *Sir John Suckling*. Copyright the Frick Collection, New York

61 Lord George Stuart, Seigneur d'Aubigny (1618–42)

Canvas, 218.4×133.4 (86×52½)

Full-length in Arcadian dress, a blue tunic and deep golden cloak with little blue bows on his boots, in a landscape, holding a crook or *houlette* and leaning against a rock on which is inscribed: *ME FIRMIOR AMOR*. A cascade of water pours from the rock, below a rose-bush, and a thistle grows beside the pool.

The sitter is almost certainly correctly identified with the third son of the 3rd Duke of Lennox, brother of the sitters in nos.44 and 48. He was killed at the battle of Edgehill, 23 October 1642, when he was in command of the Duke of York's troop in the Prince of Wales's regiment of horse: 'a gentleman of great hopes, of a gentle and winning disposition, and of very clear courage' (Clarendon, vol.II, p.368). The portrait passed, with that of his brothers (no.44) to the family of the Earl of Darnley and was bought in at the Darnley sale at Christie's, 1 May 1925 (85). 'My Lord Aubigny's picture' was recorded in the dining-room at Cobham in the inventory of 1672 (*Archaeologia Cantiana*, vol.XVII (1887), p.405); but this could also be a reference to his younger brother Ludovic.

The Arcadian convention and theatrical costume had been used earlier by Van Dyck in his portrait of Lord Wharton (fig.47); and the portrait is in the same vein as the full-length of Sir John Suckling (fig.48) in which the

Fig.47 *Philip, 4th Lord Wharton*. National Gallery of Art, Washington

mood is also sustained by a Latin inscription on a rocky ledge (M. Rogers, 'The Meaning of Van Dyck's Portrait of Sir John Suckling', *Burl. Mag.*, vol.cxx (1978), pp.741–5).

Presumably painted towards the end of the artist's life (the sitter can scarcely be less than twenty years old); the setting and the details in the foreground are painted without Van Dyck's characteristic freshness of touch. The head, however, which is slightly out of proportion, is painted with a fresh touch and considerable feeling. The unusual iconography and the motto are unexplained. The thistle and rose growing together formed one of the emblems associated with the King by Peacham in his *Minerva Britanna* (1612), 12; and in Wither's *Collection of Emblemes* (1635), bk.IV, XXIV, the thistle is seen as a symbol of affliction, which is here, perhaps, softened by association with the rose. In 1638 the sitter had married secretly Katherine Howard, daughter of the 2nd Earl of Suffolk (R.A., 1953–4, no.141).

The Earl of Darnley

62 William II, Prince of Orange (1626–50), with Mary, Princess Royal (1631–60)

(COLOUR PLATE XII, between pages 16 and 17)

Canvas, 182.5×142 (72×56)

Double full-length portrait, the Prince holding in his right hand the little Princess's left hand, on which a wedding ring has been placed.

The marriage between his only son and the eldest daughter of the King of England was an important element in Prince Frederick Henry's plans to increase the prestige and power of his family. The marriage had been under discussion since 1639 and was finally solemnized in the Chapel Royal at Whitehall on 12 May 1641: a time of tension in London, within a few days of the execution of the Earl of Strafford.

The composition can be closely dated. The Princess wears the large diamond brooch which her husband gave her on the day after the marriage. The Prince's pink costume had been made in London by David Juwery and paid for on 16 May. The Prince left London on 3 June (R. van Luttervelt, 'Het Portret van Willem II en Maria Stuart in het Rijksmuseum', *Oud-Holland*, vol.LXVIII (1953), pp.159–69). The Princess followed with her mother in February 1642. The picture had been commissioned by the Prince and Princess of Orange and in an inventory of 1654 was recorded as hanging in the Huis ten Bosch (Th. H. Lunsingh Scheurleer, 'De woonvertrekken in Amalia's Huis in het Bosch', ibid., vol.LXXXIV (1969), p.56).

In the inventory the double portrait is described as 'bij Van Dijk gemaeckt' (*Inventarissen van de Inboedels in de Verblijven van de Oranjes*, ed. S.W.A. Drossaers and Th. H. Lunsingh Scheurleer, vol.I (The Hague, 1974), p.282, no.1188). Much controversy has surrounded the picture, but it is certainly all by, or under the control of, one hand, and is, in quality, very close indeed to Van Dyck himself. On stylistic grounds there is nothing to support sugges-

63

tions which have been put forward that Lely or Hanneman might in some way have been involved. It was an exceptionally important commission, given to Van Dyck by one of his most illustrious patrons; and there is no suggestion in the early inventory that its first owners regarded the picture as anything other than an autograph work. The finished composition should perhaps be regarded as a fine example of the painter's manner in the last months of his life: extremely competent, if rather cold and hard and lacking the precision and delicacy of his best English portraits. Moreover Van Dyck had been ill since the Prince had gone back to Holland and was, during the summer, having the utmost difficulty in completing portraits of the Princess in her wedding dress for dispatch to The Hague. The technique has something of the cold, slightly harsh quality, which can be seen in the work of early imitators who may even have been working at this time in Van Dyck's studio. A number of copies and derivations are known; the best is perhaps the early copy at Bowhill (see the catalogue, *All the paintings of the Rijksmuseum . . .* (The Netherlands, 1976), p.209, A 102, for a good brief bibliography).

Rijksmuseum, Amsterdam (inv. no.A102)

63 Charles II (1630–85), when Prince of Wales

Canvas, 158.8×109.2 (62½×43)

Full-length, walking to the left, in armour with the ribbon of the Garter, resting his left hand on the hilt of his sword and his right on the head of a stick. His plumed helmet is on a roughly hewn ledge on the left.

The latest of Van Dyck's portraits of the Prince, probably to be associated with the occasion, on 9 August 1641, when a twelve-oared barge took him down to Van Dyck's studio from Whitehall. The boy had then passed his eleventh birthday and is clearly older than he was in the group painted in 1637. The walking-stick also conveys a sense of increased authority and could be compared with the stick which is so prominent in Van Dyck's portrait of the King in the hunting-field (see J. S. Held, *Rubens and his Circle* (Princeton, 1982), pp.74–6). The next stage in the Prince's iconography were the portraits painted by Dobson at the makeshift wartime court at Oxford.

The portrait must have been produced at a time when Van Dyck was sick and working under great pressure, but it is a thoroughly competent production. The head was also used for a full-length in civilian costume. The best, but not autograph, version of that variation is at Goodwood; the type was also etched in 1649, at three-quarter-length, by Hollar (P.1442).

Formerly at Raynham and sold at Christie's, 7 March 1904 (191); later acquired by Robert Benson and in 1927 given by him to Sir Hereward Wake (R.A., *British Portraits*, 1956–7, no.79; Agnew, 1968, no.61; Larsen, no.978).

Sir Hereward Wake, Bt

64 Francis Junius (1589–1677)

Panel, 24.1×21 (9½×8¼)

Head and shoulders, wearing a cloak and holding a book in his left hand.

The sitter was a native of Heidelberg and educated at Leiden. A scholar who had originally intended to pursue a military career, he had come to London c.1620 and entered the service of the Earl of Arundel as Librarian. In 1676 he retired to Oxford and bequeathed his collection of manuscripts to the Bodleian. In 1678–9 his executors presented no.64 to the Library.

In 1637 Junius had published his *De Pictura Veterum* and there exists a well-known letter from Rubens, dated 1 August 1637, thanking him for a copy of it. Equally well-known is Van Dyck's letter to Junius, dated 14 August 1636, in which he too congratulates him on 'a most learned composition', which Van Dyck had obviously seen before publication. He went on to ask Junius to favour him with a little motto which could be placed at the bottom of the engraving by Van Voerst of Sir Kenelm Digby, after Van Dyck's portrait, which was to be added to the painter's *Iconography* (Hookham Carpenter, pp.55–6).

No.64 is conceived and executed very much in the format and in the technique – monochrome on panel – which Van Dyck (and his assistants) used in preparing

64

modelli, in addition to preparatory drawings, for many of the characters in the *Iconography*; but there are some harsh passages in the portrait which perhaps make it difficult to accept the panel unequivocally as by Van Dyck. The portrait was etched by Hollar, with the date 1659 and as painted in 1640 (P.1431) (Mrs R. L. Poole, *Catalogue of Portraits . . .*, vol.I (1912), p.61; *Age of Charles I*, no.108).

The Curators of the Bodleian Library, Oxford

65 Portrait of the Artist

(BACK COVER)

Canvas (oval), 57.3×44.3 (22 9/16×17 7/16)

Head and shoulders to the right, looking towards the spectator, in a plain square band and slashed doublet.

A portrait of the artist, among pictures by him in Lely's collection ('His Own Picture in an Oval', measurement given as 55.9×45.7 (22×18)), was almost certainly a version of this type which must show the artist towards the end of his career. No.65 was bought by Mr Child at Richard Graham's sale, 6 March 1712 (41).

Something of the pressure Van Dyck was under can be detected if the face is compared with the *Self-portrait*, in the company of Endymion Porter (see the Frontispiece to this catalogue). The glance is apprehensive and the moustache has lost the dashing upward twist at the ends which is to be seen in other likenesses of the painter: the ex-Holford 'type' (Glück, frontispiece); the etched *Self-portrait*; and the *Self-portrait with a Sunflower* (page 8). An interesting, but probably not autograph, version of this type was in a private collection in 1941 (*Burl. Mag.*, vol.LXXIX (1941), p.194 and frontispiece).

The Earl of Jersey

Drawings

66 James I (1566–1625)

Black and red chalk on paper, heightened with white, on brownish paper; laid down, 21.5×17 (8½×6¹¹⁄₁₆).

Inscribed on the verso in an old hand: *Jacobus De Eerste/Koning van Groot/Brittanje/door A van Dyck.*

The old inscription has recently been discounted. The sitter is, however, without question James I. He should be compared with, in particular, the portrait by Mytens in the National Portrait Gallery (no.109; dated 1621) and the studio version at Knole.

An attribution to Pieter Soutman, put forward in the catalogue (see below) of the exhibition in 1972, is not convincing. It could not be claimed, without qualification, that the drawing is by Van Dyck, to whom it was attributed in the Fokke sale, Amsterdam, 6 December 1784 (740); but it can be suggested that it is by an artist brought up in Rubens's environment and that it shows James I, through Flemish eyes, exactly as he would have appeared to Van Dyck in the months when he was working at the English court in the winter of 1620–1, and when he had performed for the King some 'speciall service' (C. van Hasselt, *Flemish Drawings of the Seventeenth Century from the Collection of Frits Lugt . . .*, London, Paris, Bern and Brussels (1972), no.96).

Fondation Custodia (Coll. F. Lugt), Institut Néerlandais, Paris

66

67 Nicholas Lanier (1588–1666)

Black chalk, heightened with white, on blue paper, 39.2×28.5 (15⁷⁄₁₆×11¼).

A sketch for the portrait (no.6) which was almost certainly painted in Antwerp in June 1628. It is therefore one of the earliest securely dated drawings by Van Dyck in the technique he was to use so often. It is significant that the drawing was at one time in the collection of Joseph van Haeken and Ramsay. It is an early instance of the method of drawing in chalk preparatory for, or done as a record of, a painted portrait which was to be used so extensively by those two artists in the eighteenth century (National Gallery of Scotland, *Allan Ramsay, his masters and rivals* (1963), no.45). In the drawing the sitter's right hand is extended, holding a glove(?), but in the painting it rests on the hip. There is an unusually lavish use of white heightening in order to define the light area in the costume.

In the collections of Lankrink (d.1692), Van Haeken (d.1749), Ramsay (d.1784), and Lady Murray (d.1861) by whom it was presented in 1860 to the National Gallery of Scotland (*Antoon van Dyck Tekeningen en olieverfschetsen*, Antwerp and Rotterdam (1960), no.94; Vey, no.203).

National Gallery of Scotland

67

68

69

68 Charles I on Horseback with M. de St Antoine

Black chalk, heightened with white, on greenish-grey
paper, 39.8×28.3 (15⅝×11⅛)

A very hurried sketch for the great canvas painted in 1633
(no.11). It probably illustrates a stage when all the elements in the composition had been thought out and
placed in their final positions and the proportions of the
finished picture had been established. No other drawing
for a large composition survives from Van Dyck's English
years.

In the collections of Richardson (d.1745), Hudson
(d.1779), Reynolds (d.1792) and William Russell
(d.1884); purchased by the British Museum in 1885 (Vey,
no.207).

The Trustees of the British Museum

69 A Study of a Horse

Black chalk, heightened with white, on greenish-grey
paper, 42.9×36.6 (16⅞×14⅜)

A study, drawn on three overlapping sheets of paper, of a
horse in the same position as the one ridden by Charles I
in the equestrian portrait with M. de St Antoine (no.11).
The back legs are probably shortened in order to get them
on to the paper; and there is a separate study of the raised
foreleg. The position of the rider is only summarily
indicated and the details of saddle, bridle and stirrups are
omitted.

The study, which is exceptionally beautifully drawn, is
almost certainly for the King's horse, but in Brussels in
1634–5 Van Dyck painted an equestrian portrait of the
Marquis of Moncada (Glück, 420) in exactly the same
position; and the horse was also used for an equestrian
portrait of Philip IV in the Galleria Balbi di Piovera in
Genoa (*Mostra della Pittura del Seicento e Settecento in Liguria*,
Palazzo Reale, Genoa (1947), no.8). A study of the standing foreleg of the horse in this position is also in the British
Museum (Vey, no.209).

In the collections of Hugh Howard (d.1737) and the
Earl of Wicklow; acquired by the British Museum in 1874
(Vey, no.208).

The Trustees of the British Museum

70

70 Endymion Porter (1587–1649) with his son Philip (1628–55)

Black chalk, heightened with white, on brownish paper, 31.8×24.2 (12½×9½)

Inscribed in an early hand: *A. V. Dijck.*

Half-length, leaning with his right arm on a ledge and clasping the hilt of his sword with his left hand (the fingers of the left hand are separately studied). The child is placed in the foreground, in front of his father.

A sketch for the figure of Porter and his youngest son as they were to appear in the family group (fig.49) which was bought from Lely's collection by the Earl of Mulgrave, was subsequently at Buckingham House and is now in the possession of Mrs Gervas Huxley (G. Huxley, *Endymion Porter* (1959), pp.311–13, pl.6). In the painted group Porter's left hand, instead of grasping his sword, points to a statue of Pallas(?). Philip Porter had been born in 1628 and the group must have been painted soon after Van Dyck's arrival in London. See also no.87.

Endymion Porter was a cultivated and widely travelled member of the court of Charles I, to whom he was officially attached as a Gentleman of the Bedchamber. He knew a great deal about the arts and was on particularly friendly terms with Van Dyck (whom he had known on his first visit to London; see no.3) and Rubens. He was painted by Van Dyck in company with the artist himself (fig.33; and Frontispiece to this catalogue; there is much material on Porter and the arts in G. Huxley, op. cit., and

Fig.49 *The Family of Endymion Porter.* Mrs Gervas Huxley

71

in W. Vaughan, *Endymion Porter and William Dobson*, Tate Gallery (1970)).

Philip Porter, a pert, merry and attractive child, though spoiled by his grandmother, grew up into a violent young ruffian who behaved brutally to his widowed mother and died soon after being released from the Tower to which he had been committed for high treason.

In the collections of Lankrink (d.1692), Richardson (d.1745), Hudson (d.1779) and Uvedale Price (d.1829); acquired by the British Museum in 1854 (Vey, no.210).

71 François Langlois (1589–1647)

Black and white chalk on faded brown paper, 39.3×28.3 (15½×11⅛)

Inscribed later: *Van dick*.

A preparatory sketch for the painted portrait (no.10). The costume is less elaborate than it appears in the painting; the brim of the hat is not turned up; and the hound has not yet been introduced into the design.

The style of the drawing confirms the revised dating of the portrait. It is entirely consistent with the drawings made by Van Dyck in preparation for painted portraits in the second Flemish and English periods. The re-dating of the drawing was inevitable once it had been seen in the context of the exhibition *Tekeningen en olieverfschetsen*, Antwerp and Rotterdam (1960), no.63; see, for instance, C.

White in *Burl. Mag.*, vol.CII (1960), p.514. The drawing, and the subject, are fully discussed by Vey (no.169) and C. van Hasselt, *Flemish Drawings of the Seventeenth Century from the Collection of Frits Lugt . . .*, London, Paris, Bern and Brussels (1972), no.31. Acquired by Lugt in 1925, it had formerly been in the collections of Jean-Marc du Pan in Geneva; Alex-Louis du Pan, Paris (sale, 26 March 1840); F. van den Zande, Paris (sale 30 April 1855 (2971)); and Mrs A. Douchet, Paris.

72 Charles II (1630–85), when Prince of Wales

Black chalk, heightened with white, on greenish-grey paper, 34.7×23.8 (13⅝×9⅜)

Full-length, standing to the right front, in a lace cap and long 'coats'.

A preparatory sketch, almost certainly drawn from life, for the figure of the little Prince as he was to appear in the group of the three eldest royal children, painted in 1635 (no.18). In the finished picture the child rests his right hand on a spaniel and his left hand is at his side.

Acquired by the British Museum in 1874; formerly in the collections of Hugh Howard (d.1737) and the Earls of Wicklow (Vey, no.232).

72

73

73 Lady Anne Wentworth (1623–97)

Black chalk, heightened with white, on light brown paper,
34.8×23 (13$\frac{11}{16}$×9$\frac{1}{8}$)

Three-quarter-length, standing to the left, resting her
right hand on the head of a dog which jumps up at her.

A sketch for the figure of Lady Anne as she was to appear
in the family group at Wrotham Park, which was painted
by Van Dyck *c*.1635. A drawing for the figure of the
mother in the group is in the British Museum (Vey,
no.236). The group, which has been perhaps unde-
servedly neglected in the literature on Van Dyck since it
was reproduced in an article by Clare Stuart Wortley
(*Burl. Mag.*, vol.LIX (1931), pp.103–7), is now undergoing
restoration. Any discussion of the authorship of the group,
which seems fundamentally to be by Van Dyck himself,
would have to take into consideration the indubitably
autograph drawings for two of the figures.

It was through Lady Anne that the group, and the
single portrait of her mother (no.31), passed ultimately to
the present owner. She married on 11 July 1638 John, 2nd
Lord Lovelace, and in 1686 succeeded to the barony of
Wentworth. Lovelace dedicated to her his *Lucasta* (1649)
(*Antoon van Dyck Tekeningen en olieverfschetsen*, Antwerp and
Rotterdam (1960), no.116; Vey, no.237).

Victoria and Albert Museum, London

74

74 Lucy Percy, Countess of Carlisle (1599–1660)

Black chalk, heightened with white, on greenish-grey
paper, 49.8×25.8 (19$\frac{5}{8}$×10$\frac{1}{8}$)

A sketch for the full-length of the Countess of which the
original (fig.50) was painted for the Earl of Strafford (see
no.23) and is still in the Wentworth Woodhouse collection
(R.A., 1953–4, no.161). A second version (Glück, 447)
which may have been painted for Sir Henry Vane the
elder, last appeared at Sotheby's, 19 April 1967 (99). The
drawing only suggests the glance and the position of the
head and figure and was made when the sitter was wearing a less elaborate dress than the one in which she chose
to be painted; nor does it show the magnificent jewellery
the Countess displays in the finished portrait.

An intelligent, politically minded but dangerous lady:
'active and tempestuous' and 'a very pernicious instru-

Fig.50 *Lucy, Countess of Carlisle*. Trustees of the Rt Hon Olive, Countess Fitzwilliam's Chattels Settlement

75

ment'. Daughter of the 9th Earl of Northumberland (no.13), she had married the 1st Earl of Carlisle in 1617; he died in 1636. She was a close friend of the Queen – she was painted behind her, as one of Diana's attendants, in Honthorst's huge allegorical canvas at Hampton Court – and was deeply admired by Strafford whose friendship with her gave rise to scandal.

In the collections of Richardson (d.1745), Hudson (d.1779) and J. Thane (d.1818); acquired by the British Museum in 1846 (Vey, no.233).

The Trustees of the British Museum

75 James II (1633–1701), when Duke of York

Black chalk, heightened with white, on blue paper, 45×33.4 ($17\frac{3}{4}×13\frac{3}{16}$)

A study for the figure of the child in the group (no.26) painted in 1637. On the left is a rapid sketch for the position of the child as he was to be placed on the canvas; in the painting the child's hands are folded across his stomach. On the right is a study, clearly drawn from life, of the child's head.

Formerly in the collection of Richardson (d.1745) (Vey, no.239; J. Byam Shaw, *Drawings by Old Masters at Christ Church, Oxford* (1976), no.1386).

The Governing Body, Christ Church, Oxford

76

77

76 Lord Bernard Stuart, later Earl of Lichfield (1622–45)

Black chalk, heightened with white, on greenish-grey paper, 43.2×28.7 (17×11¼); the corners of the drawing have been cut.

A study for the pose and costume of the right-hand figure in no.44. The main outlines are, at this stage, established, but with a very free touch, and the rich details of the costume have been omitted. The drawing is squared for transfer to the canvas. This ensured that in the painting the main outlines and the relationship between all the parts of a complex pattern would be preserved exactly as they had been set out in the drawing.

In the collections of Richardson (d.1745), Hudson (d.1779) and Reynolds (d.1792); acquired by the British Museum in 1845 (Vey, no.231).

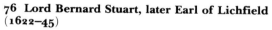

The Trustees of the British Museum

77 Thomas Howard, 2nd Earl of Arundel (1586–1646)

Black chalk, heightened with white, on brownish paper, 48×35.6 (18⅞×14)

Inscribed later: *A. V. Dyck.*

Full-length, seated in an X-frame chair of state, wearing the ribbon of the Garter and holding in his right hand a paper and in his left the Earl Marshal's baton (?).

The head could have been based on the head of the Earl in the portrait (no.21) with his grandson. The drawing, which so splendidly conveys the actual physical presence of the Earl, is traditionally thought to have been made when a family portrait group was under consideration. A drawing in the British Museum is not by Van Dyck, but may be a record of Van Dyck's intentions. In it the figure seated on the left bears a generic likeness to the figure of Arundel in no.77 and holds a baton (?) in his left hand (*Burl. Mag.*, vol.LXXIX (1941), p.190). If Fruytiers's little watercolour of 1643 records another phase in the development of this project (and it is inscribed: *An: VAN-DYKE Inv.*) it would show that Van Dyck had decided to use in it, for his principal figures, the poses he had evolved in the 'Madagascar' portrait (no.59). The figure in this drawing, seated as he is in a chair of the kind occupied by the King in the 'Great Piece' (no.7), looking down on the spectator as if he was raised on a dais like the Earl of Pembroke in the family group (fig.31) at Wilton, or the

78

79

Count of Nassau-Siegen in the huge family group (fig.34) of 1634, is not difficult to imagine as the culminating figure in another large dynastic performance.

Formerly in the collection of Uvedale Price (d.1829); acquired by the British Museum in 1854 (Vey, no.225).

The Trustees of the British Museum

78 Orazio Gentileschi (1563–1639)

Black chalk, with some grey wash in the shadows and touches of pen and sepia, 24×17.9 ($9\frac{3}{8}$×7): the principal lines are indented for transfer.

Half-length to the left, his head turned to look at the spectator, pointing with his left hand.

The sitter, a native of Pisa, had worked in Rome, where he was on friendly terms with Caravaggio. He moved to Paris, *c*.1623–4, and in 1626 settled in London under the patronage of the Duke of Buckingham, whom he had met in Paris in the previous year, at the time of Henrietta Maria's marriage. He did a considerable amount of work for the King and Queen. His most important commission was the decoration of the ceiling of the hall in the Queen's House at Greenwich. The canvases from this cycle survive, in a battered and mutilated condition, on the ceiling of the hall of Marlborough House.

Van Dyck would have known Gentileschi (and his daughter Artemisia) in London and he probably planned at that time to add his portrait to the famous series of likenesses which he had by then almost completed of some of the famous men and women of the day: the series which came to be known as the *Iconography* and in which the portraits of Van Dyck's fellow-artists outnumber other classes of sitters and provide so many vivid illustrations of the artistic circles in which he moved. To look through the engraved plates, and the preparatory drawings where they survive, is to realize what a remarkable compendium of arresting baroque patterns Van Dyck provided in this great project. The quality of the drawings of the fellow-artists have a sustained nervous brilliance in the handling of the chalk which matches and underlines an intensity and sympathy in characterization.

The drawing of Gentileschi was engraved by Lucas Vorsterman (M. Mauquoy-Hendrickx, *L'Iconographie d'Antoine Van Dyck* (Brussels, 1956), p.247, no.83; Vey, no.276). The drawing was in the collections of Hudson (d.1779), Dr Mead (d.1754), and the Rev C. M. Cracherode, by whom it was bequeathed to the British Museum in 1799.

The Trustees of the British Museum

79 Inigo Jones (1573–1652)

Black chalk on white paper, 24.5×20 ($9\frac{5}{8}$×$7\frac{7}{8}$)

Half-length to the front, looking to the right and holding a large sheet of paper in his right hand.

On the mount is a later inscription, signed by the 3rd Earl of Burlington: 'Vandyke's original Drawing, from which the Print by Van. Voerst was taken, in the/Book of Vandyke's Heads. Given me by the Duke of Devonshire'. The

111

drawing had been in the collection of N. A. Flinck (d.1723) which had been acquired by the 2nd Duke of Devonshire in 1723. His successor, the 3rd Duke, gave it to Burlington, realizing, no doubt, what such a drawing would mean to the architect who so venerated the work of his seventeenth-century predecessor and who had by then acquired the famous collection, at Chatsworth, of Jones's drawings for masques.

As architect and connoisseur and as a learned and inexhaustibly inventive designer of masques, Jones occupied a pre-eminent place in artistic circles at the courts of James I and Charles I. His travels gave him almost unique authority and a first-hand knowledge of Renaissance and contemporary art. As early as 1606 he had been described as one 'through whom there is hope that sculpture, modelling, architecture, painting, acting and all that is praise-worthy in the elegant arts of the ancients, may one day find their way across the Alps into our England' (J. Summerson, *Inigo Jones* (1966), p.29). As a draughtsman, Van Dyck considered Jones was 'not to be equalled by whatsoever great masters in his time for boldness, softness, sweetness, and sureness of touch'.

The drawing was made by Van Dyck for the plate by Van Voerst for inclusion in the *Iconography* (M. Mauquoy-Hendrickx, *L'Iconographie d'Antoine van Dyck* (Brussels, 1956), no.72). It has the combined authority and sensitivity which all the drawings of his fellow-artists, done for this scheme, display. It also has the air of having been drawn from life and is very close in type, with slight variations in detail, to the painted image of which the best, but not necessarily the original, version is in The Hermitage (Varshavskaya, pp.119–20, no.13). The portrait became the standard image of the great neo-Palladian artist. It may have provided the model for the bust on his tomb in St Benet's Church, and in the eighteenth century it was, for example, the source from which Rysbrack made his commemorative busts and statues. These are in the reverse sense from the drawing and may have been made from the print. The portrait had also been used by Hollar for the frontispiece (P.1428) to Jones's *Stone-Heng Restor'd*, published in 1655. For the place of the drawing in Jones's iconography see J. Harris, S. Orgel and R. Strong, *The King's Arcadia* (1973), pp.210–13; this volume is also the best introduction to Jones's life and achievement in all the fields in which he worked (Vey, no.271; *Age of Charles I*, no.45).

The Trustees of the Chatsworth Settlement

80

80 Margaret Lemon

Pen and indian ink wash on paper, 24.8×14.5 (9¾×5¾)

Head and shoulders to the left, her head turned towards the spectator.

Van Dyck's mistress at some time during his years in London, probably until his marriage with Mary Ruthven in 1639. She had a notoriously violent temperament and was described by Hollar as 'a "dangerous woman", a "demon of jealousy" who caused the most terrible scenes when ladies belonging to London society had been sitting without a chaperone to her lover for their portraits, and who on one occasion in a fit of hysterics had tried to bite Van Dyck's thumb off to prevent him from ever painting again' (J. Urzidil, *Hollar, a Czech émigré in England* (1942), p.47). Richard Symonds, admittedly writing some years later, records a piece of court gossip: 'Twas wondred by some that knew him thatt having bene in Italy he would keepe a M[rs] of his in his howse M[ris] Leman & suffer Porter to keep her company' (British Library, Egerton MS 1636, f.102). She appears in a (probably unfinished) portrait by Van Dyck in the royal collection (Millar, no.157) and she was probably the model for Psyche in no.58.

The drawing, which was originally in Lely's collection, was sold by the Marquess of Northampton at Christie's, 1 May 1959 (4), and was acquired by Frits Lugt. Doubts had been cast on the authorship, but the quality of the brushwork is very high and makes it probable that it is a preparatory study for a painted portrait. No autograph version of the portrait in oil is known; the best version is in

81

the possession of Lord Kinnaird; in one variant the sitter, resting her left hand on a sword, may be cast in the role of Judith. The design was also etched by Hollar in 1646 (P.1456)[1] and it was engraved by Lommelin and Jean Morin (C. van Hasselt, *Flemish Drawings of the Seventeenth Century from the Collection of Frits Lugt . . .*, London, Paris, Bern and Brussels (1972), no.33).

Fondation Custodia (Coll. F. Lugt), Institut Néerlandais, Paris

[1]The verses inscribed on this plate provide a lurid account of the sitter's activities as a high-class courtesan in London before the Civil War.

81 A View of Rye

Pen and sepia ink on white paper, 20.2×29.4 ($7\frac{15}{16} \times 11\frac{9}{16}$)

Inscribed by the artist: *Rie del naturale li 27 d'Aug^{to} 1633 – A Vand*[

Rye, on the coast of East Sussex, is built on sandstone rock which rises out of the surrounding fen. Created a royal manor under Henry III, it is one of the Cinque Ports, but its prosperity began to diminish in the second half of the sixteenth century when the harbour silted up. In Van Dyck's time it was still important as a fishing harbour, shipyard and point of embarkation for the Continent.

Four drawings of Rye by Van Dyck survive (see also no.82 and fig.51). In no.81 the view, with grasses and brambles in the foreground, is drawn from a cliff to the

north east of the town. The church of St Mary, which retains traces of a cruciform Norman church, dominates the town. Below the church, among the houses, is the fourteenth-century Landgate, the original gate to the road from London. On the slope to the left of the church can be seen the Ypres Tower, used at this date as a prison.

The drawing obviously records a special trip made to Rye. It is Van Dyck's most ambitious surviving topographical drawing. Its only recorded precursor is the drawing of Antwerp (Vey, no.287) made in 1632 on the eve of his departure for England and used in the back-

Fig.51 *A View of Rye*. Fitzwilliam Museum, Cambridge

ground of a full-length portrait of Marie de' Medici; Van Dyck's drawing of the Ypres Tower at Rye (fig.51) was used for the background of his portrait of Jabach (Glück, 316, 355). The technique, as in no.83, is essentially in the Flemish landscape and topographical traditions, intimate and affectionate in its treatment of the subject, but the touch has an individual delicacy and sensitivity; the handling becoming gradually more detailed as the eye leaves the centre of the design; the foreground is swept in with a freedom that approaches Rubens in this genre.

In the history of topographical drawing in England the very few antecedents of Van Dyck's drawings of Rye are drawings by the Flemings Van den Wyngaerde and Hofnagel. Only a few years earlier than Van Dyck Claude de Jongh produced a small number of pen and ink drawings of English scenes (E. Croft-Murray and P. Hulton, *Catalogue of British Drawings*, vol.I (1960), pp.XXIV, XXXVII-VIII, 381–4). In 1636, however, Hollar took up residence in London under the wing of the Earl of Arundel. Immensely prolific, he made a contribution of fundamental importance to the development of the English topographical tradition; but his work is oddly old-fashioned if it is set beside that of Van Dyck who, by tradition, thought little of his draughtsmanship. Hollar in fact made an adaption of no.81 and used it in his etched map of Kent (P.665; see R. R. Wark, *Early British Drawings in the Huntington Collection* (San Marino, 1969), p.31).

Formerly in the collections of Richardson (d.1745), J. van Rijmsdijk and C. Fairfax Murray (d.1919) (Vey, no.288; F. Stampfle, *Rubens and Rembrandt in Their Century*, The Pierpont Morgan Library (1979), no.32).

The Pierpont Morgan Library, New York

82 A View of Rye

Pen and dark brown ink on white paper, 16×27 ($6\frac{5}{16} \times 10\frac{5}{8}$)

Signed:]van dyck F 1634

See no.81. The view is from the south east or seaward side of the town, with St Mary's Church close to the edge of low cliffs. The drawing may have been made at the time of Van Dyck's departure from England on his short visit to his own country. It is drawn with the same fresh touch as no.81 and with the sensitivity in approaching such a subject which throws so interesting a light on Van Dyck's mind towards the end of his life (Vey, no.289).

Gabinetto Disegni e Stampe degli Uffizi, Florence

83 A Landscape Study

Pen and sepia on white paper, 18.5×28 ($7\frac{1}{4} \times 11$); there are two rectangular repaired sections on the sheet.

Signed and dated: *A:van dyck.F:1634*

A drawing of a wooded hillside with a cottage on the right. The study was probably made for use in the background of a portrait and almost certainly for a portrait commissioned during Van Dyck's months in Flanders in 1634–5. Particularly beautiful landscapes, very close in type to no.83, can be seen in the background of the portrait of an elderly lady, painted in 1634, in Vienna (Glück, 418) and in the portrait of Prince Rupert, also in Vienna (fig.17), which had been painted not long before Van Dyck came over to London.

In style and approach such a drawing is in the well-established Flemish tradition of landscape drawing in ink,

83

a technique that can be followed back through the work of, for instance, Jan and Pieter (II) Breughel or Bril to an earlier draughtsman such as Patinir; but the sense of design and the fluency of his stroke suggest that Van Dyck had been impressed, in Italy, by drawings by the Carracci and Titian.

In the collections of Lankrink (d.1692), Richardson (d.1745) and Payne Knight (d.1824), by whom it was bequeathed to the British Museum (Vey, no.294).

The Trustees of the British Museum

84 A Study of Plants

Pen and sepia and sepia wash, on white paper, 21.3×32.7 (8⅜×12⅞)

Inscribed by the artist: *on bord cron semel. Soufissels, nettels. gras. trile gras./nyghtyngale on dasy/færren*; and probably signed by him: *A. vandÿck.*

Vey (no.296) provides, on the basis of acknowledged expert opinion, suggested readings of the first part of the inscription ('on the edge' or 'on the cartoon') and a list of the plants which are probably drawn on the sheet: *Chelidonium maius* or greater celandine, *Sonchus arvensis* or corn sowthistle, *Urtica dioica* or stinging nettle, *Briza media* or common quaking grass, *Geranium robertianum* or herb robert, *Bellis perennis* or daisy and *Athyrium filix-femina* or lady fern.

A rare example of the sensitivity with which Van Dyck studied the natural world and of the pains he took in collecting material from life. Only one other such study has survived (Vey, no.297). Van Dyck had introduced plants and flowers into his compositions from an early date. In his second Flemish and English periods he frequently painted groups of plants in the foreground of his compositions. Good examples are to be seen in nos.60 and 61; the most lavish display of flowers in an English composition is in the foreground of the portrait (fig.18) of Charles I in the hunting-field, where the large plant growing on the left (probably *Arctium pubens*, the common burdock) is in very much the same form as in no.60, which suggests that Van Dyck had composed a pattern-book to be drawn on when a composition so demanded. A particularly spirited passage of foliage painting is in the foreground of no.16.

There is an obvious parallel between no.84 and studies of plants and foliage by Rubens. An almost exactly contemporary drawing by Rubens is his study of a wild cherry tree with brambles and weeds, annotated in his own hand, in the Seilern Collection (see *Rubens Drawings and Sketches*, British Museum (1977), no.198). Among later painters working in England, the artist whose plant studies have most in common with Van Dyck's is Gainsborough, whose style as a draughtsman was so profoundly influenced by Van Dyck (see his studies of burdock and mallows, J. Hayes, *The Drawings of Thomas Gainsborough*

115

84

(1970), vol.1, nos.86 and 177).

In the collections of Richardson (d.1745) and W. Russell (d.1884); acquired by the British Museum in 1885.

The Trustees of the British Museum

85 A hilly Landscape with Trees and a distant Tower

Pen and sepia ink, with grey, blue and green washes, on white paper, 22.8×33 (8$\frac{15}{16}$×13)

One of a comparatively small number of studies of landscape in watercolour which are generally accepted as late works by Van Dyck, not connected with the preparation of painted portraits but essays in landscape painting, perhaps undertaken as a relief from the increasing burden of his professional practice. In no.85 there is more interest in the sky, and the landscape is more open and rolling, than in any of the other sheets in this group, and the freedom of handling and the impromptu nature of the subject and its treatment suggest that the drawing was made out of doors. The underlying pen-work is extremely delicately applied (Vey, no.306).

As a group, the drawings are without precedent in England. They are justly regarded as 'the "incunabula" of the English art of water-colour'.

The Trustees of the Chatsworth Settlement

86 A Landscape with Trees and Ships

Pen and brown ink with colour washes and body-colour, on white paper, 18.9×26.6 (7$\frac{7}{16}$×10$\frac{1}{2}$)

The most brilliant of Van Dyck's landscapes in water-colour. The penmanship in the boats is characteristically nervous; the colour washes, in various shades of blue, green, fawn or ochre, grey and yellow are perfectly in key. Professor Hamish Miles[1] has suggested that, as a composition, the drawing is reminiscent of the background in the portrait (fig.18) of Charles I in the hunting-field. There is certainly, in the painting, a slope with trees down to a broad river or to the sea. In style also the drawing is not unrelated to the painting and could certainly be a record of the bit of country that Van Dyck wished to suggest in the background of the portrait.

Formerly in the collections of Richardson (d.1745) and Sir William Fitzherbert, from whom it was acquired in 1939 (Vey, no.304).

Barber Institute of Fine Arts, the University of Birmingham

[1]Letter written, 23 February 1982, to the compiler.

85

86

87 Philip Porter (1628–55)

Black chalk on brownish paper, 26×36 (10¼×14³⁄₁₆)

On the sheet are two studies for the figure of Philip Porter,
in the family group, which give the clear impression of
having been sketched from life and were presumably
made after the position of the child, in relation to his
father, had been established in the other and earlier drawing (no.70). On the verso is a sketch for the pose and
costume of George Porter as he was to appear in the same
group (J. Müller Hofstede, 'New Drawings by Van Dyck',
Master Drawings, vol.11, no.2 (1973), p.157).

Statens Museum for Kunst, Copenhagen

List of lenders

Her Majesty The Queen 7, 11, 22, 26, 53, 58

Barber Institute of Fine Arts, the University of Birmingham 86

Trustees of Belvoir Estate 43

The Curators of the Bodleian Library, Oxford 64

The Rt Hon The Earl of Bradford 37, 39

The Trustees of the British Museum 68, 69, 70, 72, 74, 76, 77, 78, 83, 84

The Broadlands Collection 44

Brooks Memorial Art Gallery, Memphis, Tennessee 54

The Viscount Camrose 17

The Trustees of the Chatsworth Settlement 55, 79, 85

The Governing Body, Christ Church, Oxford 3, 75

The Viscount Cowdray 10

The Earl of Darnley 61

Lady Juliet de Chair 15, 28, 32, 57

The Lord Egremont, Petworth 40, 41

Fitzwilliam Museum, Cambridge 14

Fondation Custodia (Coll. F. Lugt), Institut Néerlandais, Paris 66, 71, 80

The Duke of Hamilton 60

The Hermitage, Leningrad 20, 56

Stafford Howard, Esq 19

The Iveagh Bequest, Kenwood (GLC) 48

The Earl of Jersey 65

Kunsthistorisches Museum, Vienna 6

Rebecca Pollard Logan, USA 2

Christopher Loyd, Esq 8

Musée du Louvre 30

His Grace the Duke of Marlborough 42

Major Malcolm Munthe, MC 51, 52

The Trustees of the National Gallery 1, 16, 29

National Gallery of Scotland 67

National Gallery of Victoria 12

The National Trust, Kingston Lacy 49, 50

His Grace the Duke of Norfolk, CB, CBE, MC, DL 21, 47, 59

The Duke of Northumberland 24, 25, 36

Parham Park, West Sussex 35

The Pierpont Morgan Library, New York 81

Galleria Palatina, Palazzo Pitti, Florence 46

Private collections 9, 27, 31, 33, 38, 45

Rijksmuseum, Amsterdam 62

Statens Museum for Kunst, Copenhagen 87

L. G. Stopford Sackville, Esq 34

HM Treasury and the National Trust (Egremont Collection, Petworth) 4, 5, 13, 23

Gabinetto Disegni e Stampe degli Uffizi, Florence 82

Victoria and Albert Museum, London 73

Sir Hereward Wake, Bt 63

We are grateful to all owners for kindly allowing their pictures to be reproduced in this catalogue.
Nos. 7, 11, 22, 26, 53 and 58 are reproduced by gracious permission of Her Majesty The Queen.
The transparency of no.39 was supplied and is reproduced by permission of English Life Publications Ltd.

Index